ELECTRICITY AND MAGNETISM

PHYSICS IN ACTION

Atomic and Nuclear Physics

Electricity and Magnetism

Energy

Forces and Motion

Heat and Thermodynamics

The Nature of Matter

Planets, Stars, and Galaxies

Processes That Shape the Earth

Sound and Light

PHYSICS in ACTION

ELECTRICITY AND MAGNETISM

Heather E. Hillesheim

CHELSEA HOUSE
An Infobase Learning Company

To my physics students

Electricity and Magnetism

Copyright © 2012 by Infobase Learning

Chelsea House
An imprint of Infobase Learning
132 West 31st Street
New York NY 10001

Library of Congress Cataloging-in-Publication Data

Hillesheim, Heather.
  Electricity and magnetism / author, Heather Hillesheim.
      p. cm.— (Physics in action)
  Includes bibliographical references and index.
  ISBN 978-1-61753-099-9
  1. Electricity. 2. Magnetism. I. Title.
  QC522.H55 2012
  537—dc23
                              2011022955

Chelsea House books are available at special discounts when purchased in bulk
quantities for businesses, associations, institutions, or sales promotions. Please call
our Special Sales Department in New York at (212) 967-8800 or (800) 322-8755.

You can find Chelsea House on the World Wide Web at
http://www.infobaselearning.com

Text design by James Scotto-Lavino
Composition by Kerry Casey
Illustrations by Sholto Ainslie
Photo research by Elizabeth H. Oakes
Cover printed by Yurchak Printing, Landisville, Pa.
Book printed and bound by Yurchak Printing, Landisville, Pa.
Date printed: March 2012
Printed in the United States of America

10 9 8 7 6 5 4 3 2 1

This book is printed on acid-free paper.

CONTENTS

ACKNOWLEDGMENTS

Life takes strange turns. I never thought I would ever write a book, much less one about physics. Many people influenced those turns and helped me along this path, and I would like to thank them. First, thank you to my parents, both fantastic teachers, who instilled in me a love of learning just for the sake of gaining new knowledge. Particular thanks go to my father who helped me with some of my research by answering the most random questions. I would also like to thank Stefanie Stinchcomb who gave me the chance to try teaching physics—despite my degree in chemistry—just because I thought it would be interesting. It helped me find that physics is my favorite subject, and I will always be thankful for the opportunity. I also need to thank Elaine Wood and Pam Walker for suggesting me when asked about a "physics person." I never would have gotten this opportunity otherwise. Huge thanks go to my editor, Frank Darmstadt, for his extreme patience. From a daily email or two (or ten honestly) to helping me learn what an em dash is and when to use it, Frank was patient with my mistakes and always respectful of my knowledge. This project would not even exist without you—thank you so much.

I also need to thank my husband, Daniel, for advice on my research (even if sometimes he got overly technical) and patience when I neglected things around the house to get just a little more written. Thanks go as well to my daughter, Keely, for letting me squeeze in a few more minutes of writing by entertaining herself once in awhile. Thanks also go to Megan and Tim, two fantastic friends, for reminding me that your past helps determine who you are today and for being there through so much of mine. Final thanks go to my sister, Julie, who always knows when I need a break.

OVERVIEW

Every interaction between two particles can be attributed to one of the four fundamental forces—gravity, strong nuclear force, weak nuclear force, and electromagnetism. Gravity is the attraction between two particles. It is a long-reaching, but weak, force. Every particle exerts a gravitational force on objects around it, but the particle needs to have a great deal of mass in order for this force to be detectable. The strong nuclear force is responsible for holding the nucleus of an atom together and is the strongest of the four forces. The weak nuclear force is responsible for nuclear decay—that is, when an atom becomes stabilized by the release of particles or energy or both. Electromagnetism is the force that causes attraction and repulsion between charged particles and between magnets. This force is responsible for almost all interactions seen on the large scale—from one person shoving another to a car driving down the street.

Electricity and Magnetism explains the basics of electromagnetism, including what electricity and magnetism are and how they interact with each other. Not only is this information vital to understanding one of the four fundamental forces but also it is the foundation for most of the world's current and future technologies. Chapter 1 discusses the most basic form of electricity—static electricity—including what, on the atomic level, makes a material either a conductor or an insulator. The chapter goes on to discuss the three ways to create static electricity and to explain how that static charge can be dispersed. The first chapter finishes with a discussion on how to detect whether an object is charged using an electroscope and on how to use Coulomb's law to calculate the magnitude of a force between two charged objects. Chapter 2 continues by discussing the electrical field surrounding a charged object and by explaining how to calculate its magnitude and where it is the strongest and the weakest. The chapter examines electric potential energy within an electric field and goes on to discuss how and when objects share charge and how a capacitor is used to store charge.

Chapter 3 focuses on the second type of electricity—current electricity—in which the electrical charges are constantly flowing from one point to another. The chapter discusses the ways

Quartz crystals are piezoelectric, which means that these crystals produce a small amount of voltage when pressure is applied to them. (Courtesy of Wikipedia)

in which electrical current can be produced using electrochemical cells, generators, photovoltaic cells, and piezoelectric crystals. The chapter continues with a discussion of Ohm's law and how it can be used to show the relationship between the resistance of a conductor, the current passing through the conductor, and the voltage necessary to move those electrons. The chapter finishes by discussing electrical power along with the types of electrical work typically done and their uses.

Chapter 4 discusses current electricity, specifically when it passes through an electric circuit. The chapter discusses the nature of circuits and explains what they are, how they are measured, and the direction of electron flow. The chapter also discusses the parts of a circuit and the function of each part. Circuit diagrams are drawn the same way in every country, allowing communication across the globe about electrical circuits and their components. The chapter explains the symbols for the most common parts of a circuit and how to properly draw and read a circuit diagram. Finally, the chapter discusses various devices added to circuits as safety features to prevent fires and other electrical accidents. Chapter 5 focuses on the types of circuits, series and parallel, and describes their differences and their uses. The way current and voltage is affected in these types of circuits is explained. The chapter finishes with a description of complex circuits—those that have both series and parallel portions.

Chapter 6 begins with a discussion of the types of magnets—natural, temporary, and permanent. The chapter continues by describing the magnetic field around a magnet and the force it exerts upon certain materials within it. The rest of the chapter focuses on electromagnetism, which is the production of a magnetic field by an electrical current. The chapter describes how electromagnetism was discovered and how it is used today. The chapter also explains the three right-hand rules that are used to describe the direction of a magnetic field or force, including appropriate times to use each rule. Chapter 7 focuses on electromagnetic induction, when a changing magnetic field produces an electrical current. The chapter covers the discovery of electromagnetic induction, explains electromotive force, and examines the ways they are used in items such as generators, alternators, and transformers.

Electricity and magnetism are so much a part of our daily lives that it is vital to understand what they are and how they interact with each other. The interaction between electricity and magnetism influences how a car runs, how electronic equipment is powered, and how high-voltage electricity from a power plant is converted to a lower voltage for use in the home. *Electricity and Magnetism* should provide an understanding of what electricity and magnetism are and how they are used so that people can understand what is happening within the electronic equipment all around them.

1

Static Electricity

Static electricity is the buildup of electric charge in one location and is sometimes called *electrostatics*. Chapter 1 begins with a discussion on how electrons flow in certain materials, depending on whether these materials are electrical conductors or insulators. The chapter discusses the three ways to create static electricity—friction, conduction, and induction—and explains how to discharge, or disperse, the gathered electrons. The chapter continues with a discussion on how to determine whether an object is charged and the equipment used to detect charge. The chapter explains how to calculate the magnitude of the force that repels or attracts two charged objects using Coulomb's law. Finally, the chapter discusses the uses of static electricity in our everyday lives.

CONDUCTORS AND INSULATORS

In order to understand electricity, one must understand the parts of an atom. All atoms are made of the same three building blocks—**protons**, **neutrons**, and **electrons**. Protons are positively

1

charged and exist in the nucleus, the dense center of the atom, along with neutrons, which have no electrical charge. Electrons are much smaller than either protons or neutrons and exist outside the nucleus in several electron shells; these particles have a negative charge. An atom is electrically neutral because for every positive proton, there is a negative electron. Because protons are buried within the center of an atom, they very rarely travel, but electrons sometimes move from one atom to another, creating electrically charged materials.

A buildup of electrical charge in one location creates **static electricity**. This electrical charge comes from the electrons of the atoms all around the location. For example, when a person rubs a balloon on his or her hair, the electrons in the atoms of their hair are more attracted to the balloon and thus move to the balloon. This leaves the person's strands of hair with positive charges. The strands of hair would repel each other because of their similar charges, causing the strands to spread out as far away from each other as possible, making the person's hair stand up in all directions. As the negatively charged balloon is brought close to a wall, the electrons within the atoms in the wall are repelled, leaving the surface nearest the balloon positively charged. The positively charged wall and the negatively charged balloon attract each other, and the balloon will then stick to the wall. Eventually the electrons from the balloon spread back out into the wall and air and the attraction fades, allowing the balloon to fall to the ground.

When objects made from different materials are rubbed together, electrons are frequently transferred from one object to another; the direction of electron flow is determined by how strong of a **conductor** or **insulator** the objects are. A conductor is a material that allows electrons to flow through it easily, like metals and salt solutions. The electrons in these types of materials are only loosely bound to their atoms. The atoms in metals are so tightly packed that the electron shells begin to overlap one another; this tight configuration allows the electrons to freely flow from one atom to another, making metals good electrical conductors. In an insulator, the electrons are tightly bound to the atom, making them difficult to remove. Some common insulators are rubber,

Rubbing a balloon against hair causes the balloon to collect static electricity through friction and allows the balloon to stick to a wall. (Courtesy of Cora Black)

glass, plastic, and air. In the case of the balloon rubbed against hair, the rubber balloon is a strong insulator, whereas the hair is a much weaker insulator. Therefore, the hair gives up some of its electrons to the balloon.

CREATING STATIC ELECTRICITY

There are three ways to charge an object with static electricity—**charging by friction**, **charging by conduction**, and **charging by induction**. An object can be charged by friction when it is rubbed with an object made of a different material. This charging occurs when one object holds electrons more tightly than the other. The triboelectric series arranges materials according to how tightly the

Triboelectric Series	
Air	POSITIVE +
Human skin	
Glass	
Nylon	
Wool	
Silk	
Cotton (neutral)	
Steel (neutral)	
Amber	
Rubber	
Copper	
Styrofoam	
Plastic wrap	
Silicon	-
Teflon	NEGATIVE

atoms hold on to their electrons; materials with the most tightly held electrons are at the negative end of the series, whereas materials prone to giving up their electrons are at the positive end. In order for charging by friction to occur, the two materials must not be in the same location in the series. The further the separation of the two materials, the greater the charge that is built up. This method is the best way to charge an insulator and produces a different charge on each object. When a woman walks across a room in her socks, she can become charged by the friction between her socks and the carpet, resulting in an electrical shock when she touches a metal object and the static charge dissipates.

Charging an object using conduction requires a previously charged object to be brought into contact with another object. Because like charges repel, the charges built up in the first object are eager to spread out as much as possible into the second object, leaving both objects with the same charge. The number of charged particles is always conserved; therefore, when an object is charged by conduction, the final charge of each object is less than the charge of the original object. This manner of creating a static charge works best for conductors because the charges must be able to move easily through both materials.

Charging by induction is very similar; however, instead of touching a charged object to a second neutral object, they are

Why Does Static Electricity Build Up More in Winter?

It seems as though the buildup of static electricity occurs much more frequently in the colder months. Taking on and off a coat, getting in and out of the car, and just walking across the floor in socks are all ways that a person is likely to be shocked in the winter months but not during warmer weather. The reason lies in the fact that air tends to be less humid during the winter and that dry air is a much better insulator than damp air. Static electricity occurs in all of these examples in both warm and cold weather; however, in warmer weather, the built-up charge quickly dissipates in the damp, conductive air. In cold weather, the insulating quality of the dry air allows the static electricity to remain built up in a person's body until he or she touches a conductor, usually metal, and receives a shock.

Charges and Induction Effect

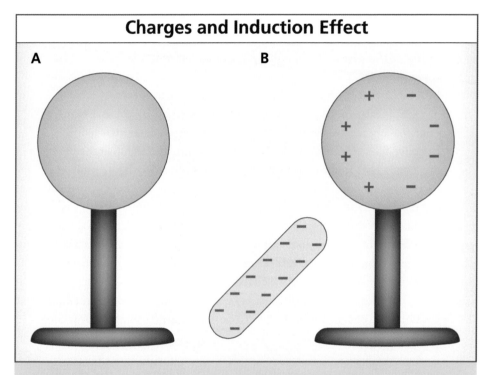

A   **B**

Bringing a charged object close to a neutral object repels similar charges while attracting opposite charges.

only brought near one another. The charges on the first object repel similar charges on the second object while attracting opposite charges. This creates a slight opposite charge on the surface of the second object that is closest to the original object.

In a situation like the one shown above, removing the original object causes the charges to spread back out, thus returning the second object to its neutral state. However, adding a **ground** allows a path for the repelled charges to leave the second object and disperse. This ground can be a wire into the Earth or a third object that starts out touching the second object but when removed takes the repelled charges away with it, allowing the second object to keeps its charge.

STATIC DISCHARGE

Static discharge, or electrostatic discharge, is the rapid and momentary movement of electrical charge from one place to another. Static electricity causes the electrical charge to build up in one location through one of the previously discussed methods. Static discharge is typically accompanied by a spark, although the spark is not always visible because of its size and the brightness of the area around its location. The feeling of an electric shock that comes with static discharge from a person is caused by the stimulation of nerves as the electrical current flows out of the person's body. The amount of built-up static electricity determines the size of the static discharge, spark, and shock; larger objects are able to store more electricity.

Lightning is an example of natural static discharge that occurs when a large enough amount of static electricity collects within clouds. The lower part of a storm cloud has a negative charge because of the gathering of electrons, whereas the top part of the cloud has a positive charge. Induction causes the ground nearest to the bottom of the cloud to gain a positive charge as the electrons within it are repelled by the storm cloud. To provide a conductive path between the cloud and the ground, the air becomes ionized, which means that the electrons are stripped from the air molecules, creating a plasma. Plasma is the less common fourth state of matter in which the object has received so much energy that it has lost all of its electrons. The electrical charge flows through the plasma, creating a lightning bolt that makes its way to the ground. The flowing charge heats the air very quickly and causes it to expand rapidly. Thunder is a shockwave of sound created by this rapid expansion of air.

Although lightning is an obvious example of when static discharge can become deadly, even much smaller shocks can be dangerous under the right conditions, such as when adding gasoline to a car. When a man gets out of a car, the rubbing of his clothes against the seat can cause a buildup of static charge, particularly in colder weather. The man getting out of his car is typically not a problem initially because he is almost certain to touch some piece

Lightning strikes are a dramatic display of static discharge. (Courtesy of Piyush Patel)

of metal—the car or the credit card reader on the gas pump for example—before he begins fueling. However, particularly in cold weather, people often get back into their warm cars while the fuel is flowing. If the man gets out again and immediately handles the gas nozzle, a spark caused by static discharge can ignite the gasoline fumes in the air, causing a fire that will continue until the gas pump is turned off. For this reason, most gas stations post signs that instruct people to touch their cars before handling the nozzle to discharge static electricity and to not return to their cars during the fueling process.

DETECTING CHARGE

To decide whether an object has become charged with static electricity, one must look for the force that a charged object applies

Van de Graaff Generators

A Van de Graaff generator is a common tool for showing the effects of static electricity. A metal sphere placed on a pedestal collects a large amount of static electricity as the generator runs. The static discharge can easily be felt by touching the sphere. Holding a hand to the sphere causes all the hair on the head to stand up straight as the strands become charged and repel each other. The American physicist Robert J. Van de Graaff (1901–67) invented the Van de Graaff generator as a way to supply the high energy needed by particle accelerators, which were used to create the foundations of particle physics.

The most commonly available type of Van de Graaff generator consists of a spherical shell resting on a column. Within the column is a belt— often made of rubber—suspended between two pulleys, one within the sphere and one in the base of the column. Metal brushes that act as electrodes are placed near the belt at both the upper and lower pulleys. The brush at the lower pulley is attached to a ground, whereas the brush at the top pulley is connected directly to the spherical shell. The bottom pulley is frequently covered in a material from the negative end of the triboelectric series, such as silicon, whereas the top pulley is covered in a material that is either neutral or from the opposite end as the bottom roller on the triboelectric series.

As a motor turns the lower pulley, the pulley begins to attract electrons from the belt; the pulley becomes negatively charged while the belt becomes positively charged. The negatively charged pulley creates an electric field around it. This field is strong enough to repel the electrons from the tip of the nearby brush, leaving them positively charged. The field also begins to ionize the nearby air, repelling the stripped electrons toward the brush tips while the positive molecules are attracted toward the negatively charged roller. The belt that is wrapped around the roller intercepts positive ions that are moving toward the roller; these

(continues)

(continued)

ions become coated on the surface of the belt, thus strengthening its positive charge.

As the positively charged belt moves into the sphere, it causes the tips of the brush to gain a negative charge as the electrons are attracted to the belt. This attracts both the positive charges from the belt and the positive ions from the ionized air. As the positive charges move into the brush, they are repelled by the belt and pushed onto the surface of the sphere. A Van de Graaff generator could ideally collect an infinite amount of charge on the sphere, but impurities in the air and other factors limit the amount of charge that can be produced. Van de Graaff generators can also produce a negative charge on the sphere when the lower roller is more positive on the triboelectric series than the belt is.

to the other charged objects that surround it. There are several ways to detect this force, such as holding an object with a known charge near the unknown object while the unknown object is able to move freely—hanging from a string. If the unknown object is attracted to the charged object, then it has the opposite charge of that known object, whereas if it is repelled, it has the same charge. If there is neither attraction nor repulsion, the unknown object does not have any charge at all.

Charge can also be detected with a lightweight, neutral object as long as the object is not a strong insulator. For example, if a man wants to know if a comb carries a charge after he runs it through his hair, he can place some strips of tissue paper on a table and pass the comb over the tissue without making contact. If the comb is charged—and it should be if the day is dry enough—charging by induction will cause the tissue to be attracted to the comb. As the comb runs through hair, the hair loses electrons to the comb, leaving it with a negative charge. Passing the comb over the tissue causes the electrons within the tissue to be repelled, leaving the surfaces closest to the comb positive, which are then attracted to the comb.

Electroscopes are the most useful way to detect charge because they can also give some indication of the magnitude of the charge. The leaf electroscope shown in the photo on page 12 is the most common electroscope. It indicates that an object is charged by the leaf and stem—or two leaves in some cases—repelling each other. This repulsion happens as charges move down from the metal cap of the electroscope through either the object touching the cap and transferring its charge—conduction—or the object being brought near to the cap and repelling similar charges—induction. Some electroscopes have a scale drawn onto a glass cover so that the deflection of the leaf can be measured; a greater deflection indicates a greater charge.

COULOMB'S LAW

Years before the French physicist Charles-Augustin de Coulomb (1736–1806) published his law in 1783, scientists understood that like charges repel each other, whereas opposite charges attract. In addition, stronger charges will cause a greater attraction or repulsion, and increasing the distance between the two charged objects will decrease the attraction or repulsion. Coulomb's law gave scientists a way to quantify this force by allowing it to be calculated in terms of newtons (N) and to thus predict the exact change in the amount of force when distances or charges are changed, as follows:

$$F = \frac{kq_1q_2}{d^2}$$

In this equation, q_1 indicates the charge on the first object, which is measured in coulombs (C), and q_2 is the charge on the second object, which is also measured in coulombs. The symbol d indicates the distance between the two objects, measured

Coulomb's law allows for the calculation of the force that repels the leaves of this electroscope. (Courtesy of Physics Department, La Sapienza)

in meters (m). Coulomb's law constant, k, is a proportionality constant, which is dependent on the medium that surrounds the two charges. When the charges are in air, k is equal to 9.0×10^9 $N \bullet m^2/C^2$. This equation assumes that the objects can be treated as a point charge, an idealized particle with an electrical charge. The force calculated using Coulomb's law is both the force on Charge 1 and the force on Charge 2 because these charges are equal but are in opposite directions in accordance with Newton's third law.

Force is a vector quantity, which means that it has a magnitude and a direction. Coulomb's law helps to calculate the magnitude—or size—of the force, but it does not indicate the force's direction. The direction of the force is dependent on the charges of each object. If the charges are the same—either both positive or both negative—then the force on each object will be in the direction away from the other object. If the charges are opposite then the force will be toward the other object. When many charges are involved the force on one object can be calculated using vector addition to sum the forces that each nearby charge exerts.

USING ELECTROSTATICS

Our modern world uses static electricity in many ways—from printing documents to trapping insects. Laser printers use static electricity to attract ink to paper and are valued for their speed and the quality of print that they produce. The central part of a laser printer is a revolving drum made of photoconductive material whose conductivity changes when struck by certain types of electromagnetic radiation. This drum starts with an overall positive charge that electrical wires usually give it. A beam of laser light draws the image or letters that will be printed on the drum, changing the charge to negative only in the areas in which the beam strikes the drum; this process produces negatively charged images on a positively charged background. The printer then coats the drum with positively charged toner particles that only the negative images attract. The sheet of paper is given a negative charge before the drum rolls over its surface. The paper's negative charge is strong enough to attract the positively charged toner away from the drum while keeping the design intact. Finally, the paper passes through a fuser in which high temperatures melt the toner particles and cause them to permanently adhere to the paper's surface. This final process is the reason why papers are always warm to the touch as they exit a laser printer.

Inkjet printers also use static electricity but in a very different manner from that of laser printers. In an inkjet printer, tiny droplets of ink, after they are given an electrostatic charge, are sprayed out of ink nozzles to strike a piece of paper. Metal plates on either side of the stream of ink are given charges to attract or repel the ink droplets in order to direct them to a specific location on the paper. Although this method of printing is slower, it has advantages in the cost of the printer and in the quality of the final images in printed photos.

Static electricity is also used to clean waste gases that industrial applications produce before these gases are released into the air. One type of electrostatic precipitator passes dirty air through a charged wire grid within a chimney. The soot, ash, and other impurities within the air become ionized in this strong electric field; this ionization process allows them to be attracted to nearby metal plates that are grounded and that may be oppositely charged to further aid the attraction. The periodic agitation or washing of the plates causes the impurities to be easily removed. This type of air purifier uses very little energy to achieve a great improvement in air quality.

Recently, research has been conducted into the static charge built up by flies and other insects as they walk across materials and fly from place to place. Nature uses this static charge to attract pollen to the insect's body and to carry it to another flower for pollination. The goal of current research is to find a way to attract statically charged insecticide powder to an insect so that it can transport the poison back to other insects. One benefit of this method is that it would limit insecticide usage to a few areas instead of being widely sprayed.

SUMMARY

In an atom, electrons can sometimes be added or removed because they orbit outside of the nucleus and are not tightly held in place. The collection of many electrons in the same place creates static electricity. While the name static means "not flowing," static electricity only occurs because electrons can move and flow from place to place. Some materials that are more likely to allow electrons to move through them are called conductors, such as metals, salts dissolved in water, and graphite. Materials that hold tight to their electrons and resist the flow of electricity are called insulators, such as air, glass, plastic, and wood. Insulators are more likely to keep a static charge because electrons do not easily disperse when they begin to collect.

Static electricity can be generated in one of three ways—charging by friction, charging by conduction, or charging by induction. When an object becomes charged by friction, rubbing two materials together generates static electricity as long as one object holds more tightly to its electrons than the other object does. As the objects are rubbed together, one object collects electrons and gains a negative charge, whereas the other object loses electrons and has a positive charge. This process is the only way for an insulator to gain an electrostatic charge. It happens, for instance, when a person rubs a balloon against his or her head—the balloon gains electrons, whereas the hair loses them.

Conduction charges a conductive material when it comes into contact with another charged object. Like charges repel each other so that when the charged object touches the neutral object, the charges spread out as far from each other as possible, leaving both objects with the same, but weaker, charge. Another way to charge conductors is through induction, whereby a charged object is positioned near the conductor. The charged object repels similar charges while attracting opposite charges and thus causing the conductor to be oppositely charged in the area that is closest to the charged object and similarly charged in the area that is furthest away from the charged object.

The production of static electricity eventually causes those electrons to spread out in a direction away from each other. The electrons in a conductor can easily move away from each other through the material; however, if the charged object is an insulator, dispersion of the electrons requires static discharge. Static discharge is a rapid, one-time movement of electrons from one place to another, usually from an insulator to a conductor. One example is when a person gets out of his or her car, particularly in the winter, and builds up static electricity through the rubbing of clothes against the car seat. When that person touches the outside of the car, or any metal, he or she receives a shock as the static electricity jumps from him or her to the metal. Lightning is one example of static discharge on a large scale; it occurs when clouds release static charge into the ground.

A charged object exerts an attractive or repulsive force on other nearby charged objects; detecting this force is how charge is detected on an object. One way to observe this force is to bring a charged or an uncharged item nearby and observe what happens. If the unknown object is charged, it will either attract or repel the charged object, depending on whether these objects have opposite or similar charges. If the uncharged object is positioned near a charged object, a static charge will be induced, and the two objects will be attracted to each other. A machine that illustrates and can even measure this attraction or repulsion is called an *electroscope*. A leaf electroscope has a metal stem with a cap on one end and a leaf—a thin piece of metal, often gold—lying against the stem at the other end. The stem is usually placed in a container, either glass or metal, with an insulator to prevent the transfer of electrons between it and the container. When a charged object touches the metal cap, the charge travels down into the leaf and the stem. Because they both have the same charge, the leaf is repulsed by the stem and lifts away from it with more displacement indicating a stronger charge.

Coulomb's law allows for the calculation of the magnitude of the force that one charged object exerts on another. It shows that the force is dependent on the charge of each object with greater charge for either object increasing the force. The equation also shows that the force decreases as the distance between the two charged objects increases. Coulomb's law also illustrates Newton's third law—the force that one charged object exerts on a second object is equal and opposite to the force exerted on it.

Static electricity—or electrostatics—is used in many different ways, including in both inkjet and laser printers. In an inkjet printer, the interaction between charged objects is used to direct charged droplets of ink to the appropriate place on a piece of paper. Laser printers draw a charge onto a roller in the image to be printed, allowing the charge to attract the oppositely charged toner. When a piece of paper slides under the roller, it is charged in such a way as to attract the toner away from the roller before it proceeds to the fuser that uses high temperatures to melt and fix the toner to the paper. Static electricity is also used to clean impurities out of the air by charging these impurities and allowing them to be attracted to plates and screens. Electrostatics may eventually put an end to the need to spray pesticides by allowing the insects to attract the charged poison and to carry it back to the rest of the population.

Static electricity explains much of the interactions between charged particles and how that interaction is used. One must first have this understanding when exploring the world of electricity and magnetism. It provides the foundation on which much of the rest of this book is built.

2

Electric Fields and Potential Energy

The electric field around a charged object is the area in which an attractive or repulsive force on other charged objects can be felt. Because this field is responsible for many of the interactions of charged particles within the world, chapter 2 begins by explaining what an electric field is and then describing how to produce and measure one. The chapter then discusses the electrical potential energy that charged particles experience when they are within the electric field. The uses of electric fields are then discussed, including the concept of grounding electrical charges. The chapter ends with an explanation of how charge is stored within capacitors and the purposes of their usage.

ELECTRIC FIELDS

An **electric field** surrounds charged objects and exerts a force on other electrically charged particles placed within the field. Coulomb's law shows that a stronger force is exerted on particles with larger charges. The strength of this field is defined as the force exerted per 1 coulomb of charge on a positive particle placed within the field and is measured in newtons per coulomb (N/C). The equation for calculating the strength of an electric field is as follows:

$$E = \frac{F}{q}$$

In this equation, E represents the magnitude of the electric field, F represents the force exerted by the field, and q represents the magnitude of the charge on the test object. The direction of the electric field is determined by the direction of the force exerted by the field onto a positive charge. Electrical fields are thus shown going from positive charges toward negative charges. If two electrical fields overlap, the resulting field is the sum of the two forces exerted per unit charge.

Lines are often used around a charged object to indicate electric fields, pointing away from positive charges and toward nega-

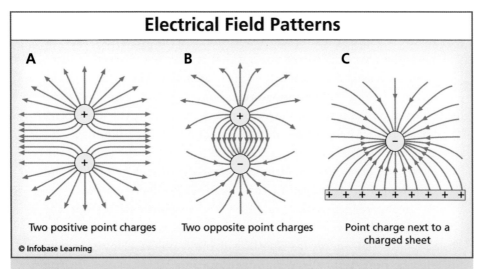

Electrical Field Patterns

A

B

C

Two positive point charges   Two opposite point charges   Point charge next to a charged sheet

© Infobase Learning

The electric field lines around (a) two positive point charges, (b) oppositely charged point charges, and (c) a point charge next to an oppositely charged sheet can be used to show the strength of the electric field at various locations.

tive charges. The closer these lines are to each other, the stronger the electric field is at that location, and lines that are further apart indicate a weaker—or absent—electric field. Although these electric field lines do not actually exist, they are useful for visualizing the electric field around an object. In diagram (a) on page 19, the electric field moves away from the charges in all directions and is strongest where the fields from the two charges reinforce each other. The electric field is very weak, or completely absent, directly between the two charges where the individual fields from each charge weaken each other. In diagram (b), the field is the strongest between the two opposite charges because their individual fields are in the same direction and produce a stronger field overall. Diagram (c) shows a situation in which one of the charged objects is a flat sheet instead of a point charge. The field is strongest in the area in which the individual fields strengthen each other—between the charge and the sheet—and weakest furthest away from the sheet.

ELECTRIC POTENTIAL

Energy is often defined as the ability to do work or the ability to use a force to cause motion through some distance. **Electric potential energy** is stored energy that is due to a charged object's position within an electric field; it is caused by the force that the electric field applies to move the charged object. The closer the charged object is to the source of the electric field, the more electric potential energy the object has. The reference point of zero electric potential energy is considered to be when the charged object is at a great distance from the source of the electric field and is no longer being moved by the force that produced by the field.

In accordance with Coulomb's law, an object with twice the charge will experience twice the force and will also have twice the potential energy as another charged object. However, the electric potential energy produced is also a factor of the electric field; describing the energy produced for any charge is more useful than describing it for each charge individually. The **electric potential difference**—the electric potential energy per charge—is most frequently used to describe the electric potential energy experienced within an electric field. Electric potential difference is measured in volts (V); therefore, it is frequently referred to as **voltage**. Although the electric potential energy of two different charges will be different, their electric potential difference will be the same when they are at the same location.

Because the point of zero electric potential energy is only a reference level arbitrarily set, calculating the change in the electric potential energy and the change in electric potential difference, ΔV, is more useful. The equation for calculating the change in electric potential difference is shown as follows:

$$\Delta V = \frac{W}{q}$$

where W represents the work done to move a charge, and q represents the magnitude of the charge.

A uniform electric field can be produced by placing two large, conductive plates parallel to each other—one plate is given a positive charge, the other is given a negative charge—which produces an electric field between the two plates that is the same everywhere except at the edges of the plates. The electric potential difference is also the same throughout the field and can be calculated using the following equation:

$$\Delta V = Ed$$

where E is equal to the strength of the electric field, and d represents the distance between the two parallel plates.

USING ELECTRIC FIELDS

In 1909, the American physicist Robert Millikan (1868–1953) used a uniform electric field to determine the charge of an electron in what became known as *Millikan's oil drop experiment*. In this experiment, oil sprayed out of an atomizer produced tiny droplets that fell over the top of a set of parallel plates between which a uniform electric field was being produced. Friction between the oil and the atomizer nozzle allowed some of the drops to become negatively charged. The top, positively charged plate had a small hole in the center through which some droplets fell. Negatively charged droplets experienced two forces as they fell through the hole—the downward pull of gravity and the upward attraction to the positively charged top plate. By adjusting the potential difference between the plates, Millikan was able to suspend an oil drop between the two plates so that the force of gravity was equal to the force of attraction to the top plate. Millikan was able to use this information to calculate the charge of a single electron as 1.60×10^{-19} coulombs.

Conductors are materials in which electrons can move with relative ease from one atom to another. When a conductor gains extra electrons, these electrons repel each other and quickly move apart so that there is as little repulsive force as possible. When this occurs, the conductor has reached electrostatic equilibrium, and no potential difference between the charges exists. This also helps to explain charging by conduction because when the two objects touch, they become one system, and charges will be moved until equilibrium is reached. When the two touching objects are the same size, the charges will distribute equally between the two. However, when one object is larger than the other, the larger object will have more charges because there is less room for charges to spread out away from each other in a smaller object. This explains why grounding works to remove excess charge from objects. The Earth is such a large sphere that it can absorb and spread out an enormous number of charges easily.

A conductor that has reached electrostatic equilibrium has several properties, including the property in which the electric field is perpendicular to the charged surface whether that surface is curved or irregularly shaped. Another characteristic of conductors at electrostatic equilibrium is that their electric fields are strongest in places in which the surfaces are the most curved. Charges spread out to reduce the electrostatic repulsion that they have for each other, which always occurs in a straight line between the two charges. When charges are along a relatively flat surface, much of this repulsive force is parallel to the conductor's surface and thus does not strengthen the electric field—which is perpendicular. However, when the charges are in a highly curved area, much of the repulsive force is closer to perpendicular, thus strengthening the electric field.

A final characteristic of charged conductors at electrostatic equilibrium is that the electric field anywhere beneath the surface of the conductor is zero. If an electric field exists beneath the surface of a conductor, this field would cause the electrons within the conductor to move and to thus make the conductor no longer at equilibrium. The electric field produced by a charged object extends from the surface of that object outward. In 1836, the British scientist Michael Faraday (1791–1867) further explored this characteristic with his invention of a Faraday cage. A Faraday cage consists of a container made of a conductor that shields the interior of the container from electric fields. Faraday dramatically demonstrated this by constructing a room within a room in which the inner room was covered with a metal foil and the walls of both rooms were charged. Faraday sat within the inner room with an electroscope while sparks flew between the surfaces of the outer and inner rooms, but he was unable to detect any electric field. The excess charges collected by the inner room existed only on the outer surface of its walls.

STORING CHARGE

Capacitors are devices that can store electrical energy, enabling it to be released and used at a later time. Batteries store electrical energy in the sense that they contain the components to produce new energy, whereas capacitors store energy that has already been produced. The German physicist Ewald Georg von Kleist (1700–48) and the Dutch scientist Pieter van Musschenbroek (1692–1761) invented the capacitor within a few months of each other in 1745–46, although Musschenbroek's invention was better known and is frequently credited as the first capacitor. Early capacitors were called *Leyden jars*—after the University of Leyden where Musschenbroek worked—and consisted of a glass jar lined inside and outside with a metal foil. A metal wire or rod

When Lightning Strikes a Car

Although being in a car that is struck by lightning is almost certainly a frightening experience, it is unlikely to pose a physical danger. Despite popular belief, this unlikelihood of danger is not due to the rubber tires on a car. Because the lightning bolt has already traveled through several miles of air—an insulator—a few inches of rubber will not deter it. Instead, the car's mostly metal shell acts like a Faraday cage by keeping the electric charge on the outside surface of the car and thus protecting the passengers within. From the outside of the car, the lightning travels to the ground, either passing through the air between the car and the ground or passing through the rubber tires. Although lightning strikes leave passengers unscathed, the car itself does not typically receive the same protection. The extreme heat of a lightning strike can ruin paint, melt electrical wires, or cause other damage, although some cars do survive strikes without any major damage.

On average, a commercial airplane is struck once a year by lightning, although the shell of the airplane protects passengers in the same way that the shell of a car does. However, the melting of wires or the heating and ignition of fuel has caused deadly plane crashes. In the 1970s and 1980s, National Aeronautics and Space Administration (NASA) scientists researched ways to prevent this kind of damage to an aircraft, and since these protective measures have been implemented, lightning strikes on airplanes have become significantly less dangerous.

was passed through an insulating cork in the mouth of the jar to touch the metal lining inside of the jar. As electricity was applied to the metal wire or rod, the two foils developed equal but opposite charges, thus producing an electric field within the insulating glass jar that allowed electrical energy to be stored.

Modern capacitors are much smaller and consist of two metal plates that are separated by an insulator called a *dielectric*. The insulator can be made of many different materials, depending on the application of the capacitor. Capacitors are described by their **capacitance**, which is the ratio of the electric charge on each plate to the potential difference between them as shown in the following equation:

$$C = \frac{q}{\Delta V}$$

In this equation, C is for capacitance, which is measured in farads in honor of physicist Michael Faraday. One farad of capacitance indicates that the capacitor holds a charge of 1 coulomb with a potential difference of 1 volt. A 1-farad capacitor would have to be relatively large; therefore, capacitance is often measured in microfarads—millionths of a farad.

Capacitors can be many different sizes; larger capacitors have a greater capacitance. They can be put to many different uses in

Capacitors come in many different shapes, sizes, and colors; however, they are all used to store charge. (Courtesy of Wikimedia)

How Stud Finders Work

Heavy items that are hung on walls or shelves that are attached to walls must be anchored to wall studs. Wall studs are vertical pieces of wood—or sometimes metal—under the drywall that help support and frame the room. Nails that are inserted into walls between the studs have only the drywall to secure them—only empty space exists behind the walls in these areas. Before the advent of electronic stud finders, locating studs was a tedious process. A person could tap along the length of the wall and listen for a difference in sound between the hollow spaces and the studs. A pivoting magnet could be used for its attraction to the metal nails within studs. A person could also look for places in which the baseboards have been nailed into the studs. All of these methods involve an amount of luck and guesswork and are potentially time consuming.

Electronic stud finders were invented in the 1970s to make the process used to locate wooden studs much simpler. These stud finders have a capacitor plate within them; they measure the dielectric constant of the wall as they are passed along the surface of the wall. The dielectric constant of a material describes the capacitance that a capacitor would have when that material was used as the insulator between the capacitor plates. Materials that are denser—like the wood within wall studs—have a higher capacitance and, therefore, a higher dielectric constant. Although some newer stud finders have begun to use radar to detect studs within walls, an internal capacitor electronic stud finder is still the most common tool used for this job.

modern electronics. Unlike batteries that release electrical energy slowly over time, capacitors can release all of their stored electrical energy at once. This ability makes them useful when bursts of electricity are needed, such as in a camera's flash. When the flash is turned on, the battery charges the capacitor so that when a picture is taken, a sudden rush of electrons causes the light to flash brightly. The ability to store large amounts of voltage even when

Electronic stud finders use changes in capacitance to detect the presence of studs within walls. (Courtesy of Zircon.com)

connected to a low-voltage battery means that capacitors must always be handled with care. They can retain their charge for hours after being disconnected from a power source.

SUMMARY

The electric fields that surround charged objects are responsible for the interactions between multiple-charged objects. This field exerts an attractive or a repulsive force on other charged objects; this force is either strong or weak depending on the magnitude of the charge on the object in question. Therefore, defining the strength of an electric field by the force exerted on the object, per coulomb of charge that the object has, is simpler than defining it by the strength of the force itself, as this strength changes depending on the charge. The strength of the electric field will be the same for any amount of charge located at the same location. Because the direction of the electric field is in the same direction as the force exerted by the field on a positive charge, so it will always go away from positive charges or toward negative charges. Electric field lines are often used to visualize the electric field surrounding an object. The closer these lines are to one another, the stronger the electric field is at that location. These lines can be used to show that the area between two point charges will have the strongest electric field when the points are oppositely charged and the weakest electric field when the points have the same charge.

Electric potential difference is how the electric potential energy—an object's ability to move because of its position within an electric field—per charge is measured. Because the point at which an object has zero electric potential energy is a reference level and is different for each object, discussing the change in potential difference an object undergoes when it moves is more useful. Electric potential difference is measured in volts (V), and the measurement is often referred to as the voltage of a charged object.

When two metal plates are placed parallel to each other and given equal but opposite charges, a uniform electric field is created between the plates. Robert Millikan used this type of field to calculate the charge of an electron in his oil drop experiment. In this experiment, a charged drop of oil was held suspended between the two plates when the electrical attraction to the upper plate was completely balanced by the downward pull of gravity. Knowing that these two forces must be equal allowed Millikan to calculate the charge of the electrons within the drops of oil.

When a conductive material becomes charged, it quickly reaches electrostatic equilibrium, whereby all of its charges are spread out to reduce the repulsive forces between them as much as possible. Materials at electrostatic equilibrium have several unique properties, including the property in which the electric field is always perpendicular to the surface of the object even when that surface is irregular. The electric field for these materials is also the strongest at the points on the surface where the amount of curvature is the greatest and weakest where the amount of curvature is the least. In addition, no electric field exists beneath the surface of a conductor at electrostatic equilibrium, which means that the charge is on the outer surface of the material. A conductor used to make a container results in a Faraday cage in which the inside of the container is protected from any electric field.

Capacitors store electrical energy and allow it to be released in a single burst or more slowly over time. Modern capacitors consist of two small metal plates with an insulator called a *dielectric* between them. This insulator is the area in which the electrical energy is stored; using different materials for the dielectric can change the functionality of the capacitor. Capacitance measures the ratio of the charge on each plate to the potential difference between them; it is measured in farads. Because this ratio is typically rather small, scientists often use the smaller unit, microfarads, to describe capacitance.

Electric fields and electric potential difference are vital to the understanding of static electricity and are used when describing the flow of electrons in current electricity. These concepts will aid in the understanding of electrical circuits and electromagnetism discussed in later chapters. Although these first two chapters have only discussed the buildup of electrons in one place, the knowledge gained here will help the reader understand the rest of the chapters in this book.

3

Current Electricity

Although static electricity involves electrons gathering in one location with possible jumps from one place to another during discharge, current electricity is the continuous flow of electrons along a path. Chapter 3 initially focuses on several different ways to cause electrons to flow, including batteries, photovoltaic cells, and generators. The chapter continues with a discussion on the proper terms and measurements used to describe the flow of electricity and some terms applicable to all types of electricity. The chapter then explains Ohm's law—a mathematical relationship between the resistance, current, and voltage of an electrical path. Finally, the chapter explains electrical power, its applications, and methods used to measure it.

MAKING ELECTRONS FLOW

Flowing electrons create **current electricity** that enables lights to turn on when a switch is flipped, but what causes these electrons to flow? A potential difference must be created to cause electrons to flow. This potential difference is set up by gathering negative charges at one end of a wire and removing them from the other.

This process creates a positive and a negative end, which creates an electric field to exert a force to push electrons from the negative to the positive end. However, eventually the electron imbalance would be corrected once the same number of electrons is at each end and the electric current ceases to flow. In order to keep current flowing, this imbalance must be kept up to continually transfer electrons from one end to the other, which is why electrical paths must be closed. As in all things, energy must be conserved; therefore, the electrical energy created must be converted from some other type of energy.

One of the most common ways to create this electron imbalance is through an **electrochemical cell**—more typically called a battery. In 1780, Italian physicist Luigi Galvani (1737–98) found that when two different types of metals were connected and came in contact with different parts of a nerve in a frog's leg, the leg would move. In 1791, Alessandro Volta (1745–1827), the Italian physicist for whom the unit "volt" was named, showed that placing a piece of cloth or cardboard that had been soaked in salt water in between two different pieces of metal produces an electric current. This current occurs through an oxidation-reduction reaction between the two metals in which one metal loses electrons that the other metal gains, thus creating a flow of electrons. This process of creating an electrical current between two metals has become known as the *galvanic* or *voltaic cell*. Chemical energy from the reaction is used to produce electrical energy. In 1800, Volta stacked several of these cells on top of each other, creating the first battery.

Modern electrochemical cells can be one of two types—a wet cell or a dry cell. A wet cell is made up of two half cells—a metal electrode placed into an electrolyte solution. One electrode loses electrons that travel along a wire to the other electrode that gains electrons. Ions of the electrolytic solution travel along a salt bridge to the other solution to keep the electron imbalance going. These types of electrochemical cells are characterized by using a liquid electrolyte and are commonly used in car batteries. The electrolyte in a dry cell is a paste that only has enough moisture present to allow current to flow. The physical state of this electrolyte (the

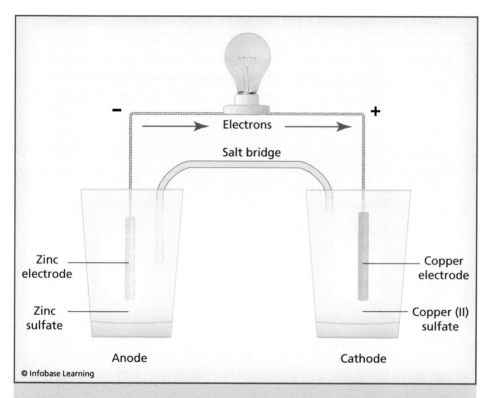

Electrons

Salt bridge

Zinc
electrode

Copper
electrode

Zinc
sulfate

Copper (II)
sulfate

Anode

Cathode

© Infobase Learning

The zinc electrode loses electrons while the copper electrode gains them, causing the electrons to flow through the wire and light up the light bulb. The electrons return to the zinc solution through ions that travel along the salt bridge.

paste) makes dry cells much more portable and safe because they have no harmful solution that could leak. Most modern batteries, such as AA batteries, are of this type. These batteries still consist of a positive and a negative electrode that exchange electrons through an electrolyte.

A **photovoltaic cell** is another way to produce the potential difference necessary for electricity to flow. A photovoltaic cell converts light energy into electrical energy and is more commonly called a *solar cell*. Light consists of a stream of photons—packets of energy—and when these photons strike certain materials, they release electrons, thus allowing current to flow. Photovoltaic cells were first used to power satellites in space, but they are now used in many applications from powering calculators to providing electricity for homes.

The **piezoelectric effect** describes the way in which certain types of crystals produce a potential difference when they are put under mechanical strain, such as being hit or placed under pressure. A final way in which an electrical current can be produced is through the use of a generator, which converts mechanical energy into electrical energy. Chapter 7 will discuss generators in depth as it examines the process of electromagnetic induction.

OHM'S LAW

It is important to be able to describe electricity quantitatively with numbers that describe its energy and speed. In current

Many calculators have photovoltaic cells that allow them to be powered by solar energy. (Courtesy of Quality Management Services)

electricity, the term *voltage* is often used instead of potential difference to describe the energy per charge within an electrical path, although the words are interchangeable. The rate at which the electrons flow through this path is called the **electric current**. Since charge is measured in coulombs, the units of measurement for current are coulombs per second, or ampere (A), frequently shortened to "amp."

(continues on page 36)

Piezoelectricity

In the 18th century, several scientists used their knowledge of the way in which some materials produce electricity when exposed to temperature changes to predict that mechanical stress—pushing or pulling—on a material could cause it to produce electrical current. Unfortunately, these earlier scientists were unable to demonstrate or prove their theory. It was not until 1880 that French physicists Jacques Curie (1856–1941) and Pierre Curie (1859–1906) were able to demonstrate this theory and thus named it the *piezoelectric effect*. These two brothers focused on the shape of certain crystal structures to determine how to produce electricity through the deformation of that structure. Some of the crystals that they discovered had piezoelectric properties were quartz, topaz, cane sugar, tourmaline, and Rochelle salt. When the converse piezoelectric effect was suggested, the brothers quickly proved it by showing that these types of crystals would deform or change shape when an electric current was passed through them. Piezoelectricity is one of the few links between electrical physics and mechanical physics because it links movement and electricity.

Any solid can have a crystal structure as long as the molecules within it make regular, repeating patterns. In a crystal structure the smallest repeating unit is called the *unit cell*. In many crystals, this unit cell is symmetrical, effectively cancelling out any imbalance of electrons within the molecule. The unit cells within a piezoelectric crystal are nonsymmetrical, which allows for the creation of dipoles—a slight positive charge at one end and a slight negative charge at the other end—within the crystal structure. The unit cells within a crystal structure naturally scatter themselves so that their dipoles are in many different directions, thus cancelling out one another's charges. However, when the crystal is squeezed or stretched in some way, the dipoles line up and create a potential difference and electricity. When the crystal is deformed in the opposite direction, electricity still flows but in the converse direction. For the reverse effect, the electric current passing through the crystal causes the dipoles to line up.

Electric lighters use the voltage produced by the compression of a piezoelectric crystal to ignite gas to produce a flame. (Courtesy of Wellpromo.com)

For many years after piezoelectricity was understood, it remained unused outside of laboratories until piezoelectric transducers—devices that convert one type of energy into another—were used for sonar during World War I to detect submarines. These transducers converted electrical energy into sound energy by causing the crystals to rapidly change shape, thus creating a pressure wave that produced sound. Since then, piezoelectric crystals have been used in many different ways, particularly since the development of more efficient, manmade piezoelectric ceramics and other materials. One common use of piezoelectricity currently is in electric lighters. A piezoelectric crystal lies underneath the button of an electric lighter; when the button is compressed, an electric current is produced that applies a spark to the flammable gas within the lighter and ignites it.

(continued from page 33)

In the early 1800s, German physicist Georg Simon Ohm (1789–1854) became a high school mathematics and physics teacher after receiving his doctorate. In the school's physics laboratory, he began experimenting with the recently developed voltaic cell. Through his experiments, he developed his law of proportionality between the current and voltage within an electrical path. He published his results, which became known as Ohm's law, in his 1827 book *Die galvanische Kette, mathematisch bearbeitet.* This book investigates the galvanic circuit mathematically. Although a complex version of Ohm's law appears in this book, the following equation is the more simplified version used today:

$$I = \frac{V}{R}$$

In this equation, I represents current, V represents potential difference, and R represents the **resistance** of the material to the flow of electrons, measured in ohms (Ω).

Although this equation is one of the early foundations upon which the study of electricity has been based, German scientists at the time did not welcome or even believe it when Ohm first published his work. The German Minister of Education said that ". . . a physicist who professed such heresies was unworthy to teach science." Most of these scientists believed that truths about the nature of science should be discovered through deduction alone, not through experimentation. Ohm even resigned his teaching position as a result of the discredit he was receiving. The scientific community did not accept Ohm's work until the 1840s when he finally received the credit he deserved for his experimentation.

Ohm's research also led to the identification of resistance as a physical property of all materials, with the exception of the later discovery of superconductors that have no resistance at all. The resistance of an object can be defined as the ratio of the voltage passing through the object to the current. Conductors have much less resistance than insulators; however, even in electrical wiring, the resistance of the wires acts analogously to friction—slowing down the current and losing electrical energy to heat. For most materials called *Ohmic materials*, resistance is a fixed quantity, no matter the voltage or current involved. A few special materials have a resistance that changes as the voltage or current changes.

The resistance of a material is a function of that material's resistivity—its natural resistance to the flow of electrical current. The cross-sectional area of the material and the material's length both also influence the material's resistance, with greater areas and shorter lengths having less resistance. Resistance in a metal is caused by the motion of ions and by the scattering of electrons within the material. A greater cross-sectional area provides more electrons available to carry the current, whereas a longer length provides more time for electrons to scatter.

ELECTRIC POWER AND USING ELECTRICAL ENERGY

Power is a measurement of the rate at which work is done or the rate at which energy is transferred. **Electric power** is the rate at which electrical work is done—the moving of electrons being work—or the rate at which energy is changed into electrical energy. Electrical power can be calculated using the equation from classical mechanics, where P represents power, W represents work, and t represents the time in seconds, as follows:

$$P = \frac{W}{t}$$

However, because the work involved is the moving of electrons and because the rate at which those electrons move is current, the following equation is typically more useful for electrical power:

$$P = IV$$

The units of measurement for power are joules per second or watts (W).

Electrical energy can be used in many different ways. Some devices are designed to change electrical energy into another

Electric Eels

The electric eel—*Electrophorus electricus*—is a South American knifefish capable of producing 500 volts with its body. Electric eels have long, slender bodies with all of their internal organs in their heads. About 80 percent of their body is an electricity-producing tail. These eels have no fin along the top of their bodies; instead, they have a long fin along most of the bottom of their body, which they use to propel themselves through the water. Electric eels typically live in muddy, shallow water in freshwater floodplains, swamps, and creeks. These creatures take the majority of their oxygen from the air by frequently breaking the water's surface to breathe. The electric eels' already poor vision further deteriorates with age. They must therefore use the electrical current they produce to navigate the muddy waters where they live.

Electric eels have three electrical organs within their long tails—a large one and two smaller ones. The large organ and one of the small organs are responsible for the high-voltage current that electric eels can produce to either stun their prey or scare off predators. These organs contain around 5,000 to 6,000 electroplaques—small, disc-shaped cells that produce a tiny amount of voltage. The electroplaques are stacked together like batteries in series so that when the nerves of the electric eel send impulses to activate them, the small amount of voltage, around 0.1 volt, produced by each allows a current to flow through the eel. Because electric eels live under water, the surrounding water does provide

type of energy, such as motors that change electrical energy into mechanical energy or car horns that change electrical energy into acoustical energy. However, some energy is always lost to heat in these processes because of the resistance of the objects within the electrical path. Sometimes this loss is purposeful, such as in incandescent light bulbs. As electrical current passes through the tungsten filament of an incandescent bulb, the resistance of

Electric eels produce an electric shock along their skin. (Courtesy of Wikimedia)

extra paths for the electricity to flow. These extra paths increase the voltage but reduce the current so that the eels' shock is more likely to stun than to kill.

the filament causes the current to slow down, converting some of the electrical energy into thermal energy. As the filament grows hot, it begins to glow and produce light; higher-wattage light bulbs convert more electrical energy into light energy.

Other devices are also designed to lose as much electrical energy to heat as possible, such as electric heaters, hot plates, and curling irons. All of these devices use large resistors within them

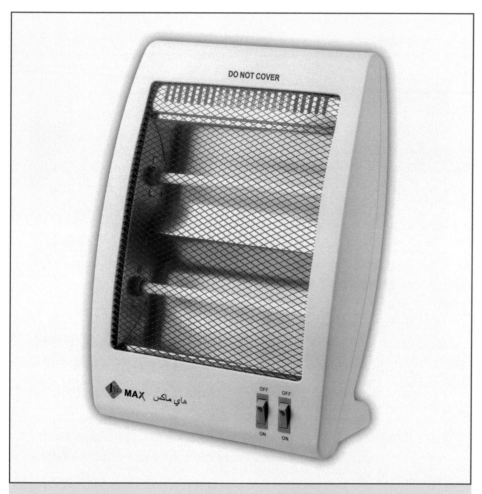

Electrical heaters convert electrical energy into thermal energy. (Courtesy of HiMax)

to convert electrical energy into thermal and only differ in how that energy is delivered. The following equation calculates the total amount of energy converted into thermal energy:

$$E = Pt = I^2Rt$$

In this equation, E represents the thermal energy (measured in joules (J)) produced, which can be calculated either by multi-

plying the power used by the time or by multiplying the current squared by the resistance and by the time elapsed.

In some situations, any loss of electrical energy is undesirable, such as when energy is being transferred long distances from a power plant to homes. In these cases, wires with the lowest resistance and widest cross-section possible are used to help reduce the amount of electrical energy lost to heat in the surroundings. Power lines carry high-voltage electrical energy because this keeps the current low and helps to reduce the amount of electrical energy lost. For this reason, the voltage carried by these lines must be converted into a form that household electronics can use before it enters a home.

The term *power company* is somewhat misleading because a power company provides electrical energy, not power. The unit most commonly used by electric companies to bill customers is the **kilowatt-hour** (kWh). This is not a measurement of the number of watts used per hour; instead, it is a measurement of the kilowatts used—1,000 watts equals 1 kilowatt—times the number of hours the power was used. Because the unit "watts" is actually joules per second, multiplying this unit times the time elapsed in seconds, leaves the unit "joules," which is the appropriate unit for measuring the amount of energy delivered.

SUMMARY

Current electricity is responsible for powering almost all of the electronics in the world from air conditioners to televisions. A potential difference must be created to produce current electricity, and a closed path must be provided for electrons to flow. Some source of energy must be converted into electrical energy so that these electrons can move. The most common way to create this potential difference is with an electrochemical cell—a device that converts chemical energy stored in the bonds of atoms and molecules into electrical energy. An electrochemical cell produces an oxidation-reduction reaction that causes one compound to lose electrons while the other compound gains electrons. This movement of electrons creates the potential difference needed to produce current electricity. There are two types of electrochemical cells—dry cells and wet cells—that are characterized by the physical state of the electrolyte through which electrons flow. The electrolyte in a dry cell is a paste that has only enough moisture to allow electrons to flow, whereas the electrolyte in a wet cell is a solution that can pose problems in terms of harmful leakage.

Another way to create the necessary potential difference is with a photovoltaic cell. These cells use light-sensitive materials to convert light energy into electrical energy. A piezoelectric crystal converts mechanical energy into electrical energy by applying stress to the crystal. These crystals also work in the reverse direction, whereby an electrical current causes the crystal to deform its shape. Generators can also be used to convert mechanical energy into electrical energy through electromagnetic induction.

In order to describe the flow of electricity, several measurements can be taken. Current is used to describe how fast the electrons flow along their electrical path and is measured in amperes, or amps. Voltage and potential difference are two terms that describe the energy per charge available to move the electrons and are measured in volts. German physicist Georg Ohm experimented with electricity when electrochemical cells were first invented and formulated Ohm's law. This law explains the relationship between current and voltage and introduces a new value—resistance. Resistance is a material's natural opposition to the flow of electrons and is measured in ohms. Ohm showed with his law that current and voltage are inversely proportional to each other—when one increases the other decreases. He also showed that increasing the resistance of a material makes the current smaller and the voltage larger. Although the scientific community at the time did not initially receive this law well, it has become a cornerstone of electrical physics.

Electrical power is a measurement used to describe how fast electrical work is done, or how fast energy is converted into electrical energy. As energy is converted into electrical energy, some is lost to heat because of the resistance of the materials. At times, this loss is purposeful, such as in light bulbs, heaters, and hair dryers. In these cases, materials with high resistance are used to increase the amount of energy converted to thermal energy. However, when electrical energy must be carried through wires to peoples' homes, resistance must be kept to a minimum to decrease the amount of energy dissipating into the surroundings. Large wires with low resistance are used to decrease the amount of energy, and high voltage and lower current electricity is transmitted.

Most of the electronics experienced in daily life are run by current electricity. Within these electronic devices are electronic paths through which electrons flow. Understanding the terms used to describe this flow of electrons and the methods used to induce the electrons to flow is critical knowledge needed to grasp how these devices work. Chapter 4 will discuss the electrical path needed for the flow of electrons in more detail.

4

Electric Circuits

Chapter 4 focuses on electrical circuits—the path for electrons to flow—including the types of circuits. The chapter continues by discussing some of the most common parts of a circuit, such as lights, resistors, and batteries. Circuit diagrams are a universal way in which to show how to build an electric circuit. This chapter discusses some of the specific symbols used when drawing circuit diagrams and the rules that must be followed to draw one so that the symbols will always look the same. Finally, the chapter describes safety devices used in circuits from when and where to use them to how they function.

WHAT IS A CIRCUIT?

An electric circuit is the closed path through which electrons flow to deliver electrical energy to an object or objects, such as the wiring that allows lights to turn on in a house. The path is called *closed* because it begins and returns to the same place—the source of the electrons. Many different devices, including those introduced in chapter 3 (electrochemical cells, photovoltaic cells, and generators), can be used as the source of the electrons. The electrons must flow back to the voltage source to maintain the potential difference between the positive and negative terminals. The entire path of the circuit must be made of conductive materials. If any portion of that path breaks or does not allow electrons to flow through it, that entire path within the circuit stops working. A light bulb burns out because the thin filament within it eventually breaks, thus causing the electron flow through the bulb to cease.

Two types of current can flow through a circuit—**direct current (DC)** and **alternating current (AC)**. The electrons in direct current only flow in one direction. Although these circuits are easier to set up, a greater amount of energy is lost because the electrons travel the entire distance of the path. Alternating current allows the direction of the current to change rapidly back and forth between directions, allowing it be transmitted over much larger distances with less loss. Direct current is produced by batteries and is typically used within electronic devices such as cell phones and cameras, whereas alternating current is the type of current present within homes and business.

The components of a circuit can either be in series or in parallel with each other. In a **series circuit**, the components are in the same path. Because this type of circuit requires fewer wires, it is cheaper to produce; however, if one component in the series stops working, the entire series no longer receives its flow of electrons and ceases to work. A **parallel circuit** has more than one path for electrons to flow, which allows one component to stop working without preventing others from continuing to receive electrical current. Although parallel circuits are more expensive to produce, they are more practical for situations in which many components share the same circuit.

PARTS OF A CIRCUIT

Although a circuit contains many different possible components, this section will cover some of the most commonly used parts of a circuit. All circuits must have two essential parts—conducting wires through which the electrical current can travel and a source

Conventional versus Charge Current

Early electrical physicists like Benjamin Franklin (1706–90), the American famous for his work with electricity, assumed that the flow of positive charges flowing created electricity—this is why the direction of electric forces and fields is assuming interactions with a positive test charge, or the flow of positive charges. Thus, the direction of current was shown to travel from the positive terminal and toward the negative; this directional flow is called *conventional current*. Unfortunately, further research, such as the work done by British chemist Ernest Rutherford (1871–1937), that indicated that protons were tightly held in the nucleus of an atom showed that it was typically electrons that carry electrical energy. Electrons flow from the negative to the positive terminal; this flow is called *charge* or *electron current*. College physics classes and engineers still use conventional current even though it was shown to be wrong. This book will use conventional current as well on the basis that some symbols used in circuit diagrams and the right-hand rules explained in chapter 6 rely on the direction of conventional current.

for potential difference. The two most commonly used voltage sources are electrochemical cells—batteries—and generators. Batteries are typically more compact and thus more useful in portable electronic devices, whereas generators are often used when larger amounts of electricity are needed. Homeowners may have generators for powering refrigerators and electric heaters during power outages, and hospitals have some backup generators to keep specific equipment working. Circuits also may contain a capacitor—a device that stores charge—that allows the stored charge to be released as one burst after another instead of a steady stream of electrons.

Light bulbs, a common feature of circuits, are used either for illumination (their main purpose) or as a way to visually see that the circuit is functioning properly. **Light-emitting diodes** (LEDs) are replacing lights in many circuits because they use less energy and last longer. Switches are a way to open and close the circuit in order to turn the circuit off and on. When the circuit is open—meaning that there is a break in the path—the electron flow is stopped, and the circuit is turned off. Although unhooking a wire also turns a circuit off, switches are more convenient, particularly in situations in which the circuit is hidden, such as in the wiring for lights in homes. A **transistor** is a semiconducting device that changes the current that flows through it. Transistors are commonly used to amplify the current within a circuit, thus outputting more power than what they take in.

(continues on page 50)

Light-emitting diodes (LEDs) use a semiconductor to produce a bright light while using less electricity. (Courtesy of Kinetic Chromatherapy.com)

Light-Emitting Diodes

Although scientists discovered in the early 1900s that passing an electric current through some specific materials could produce light, it was many years before that electroluminescence was put to practical use. In 1962, American engineer Nick Holonyak, Jr. (1928–), invented the first practical LED that produced light within the visible spectrum, red, earning himself the nickname "the father of the light-emitting diode." For the first several years, LEDs were extremely expensive to produce—around $200 per light—and thus went largely unused. Eventually, industry began the mass production of LEDs while searching for better and cheaper materials for their construction. Present-day LEDs come in most wavelengths of the visible, infrared, and ultraviolet spectrums.

An LED is one of the few devices within a circuit that is directional, meaning that it must be inserted into the circuit in a specific way in order to operate. All diodes share this property, including diodes that do not produce light. Diodes contain a semiconductor that is a poor conductor and other atoms that are added as impurities—a manufacturing process called *doping*—in order to improve the material's conductivity. Semiconductors can be doped in one of two ways for use in a diode. An N-type material is given extra electrons in the impurities added to it, giving it a negative charge. A P-type material is given electron holes—atoms with empty spots in their electron shells for the addition of more electrons—effectively giving it a positive charge.

A diode consists of an N-type material bonded to a P-type material with electrodes on each end. Even when no electricity is applied, some of the free electrons from the N-type material make their way to the P-type material. These free electrons release energy as they fill the vacant holes in an electron shell within the P-type material. This process creates a depletion zone between the two materials where the semiconductor has returned to its insulating state. In order to enable electricity to flow through a diode, the electrode on the N-type end of the semiconductor must be connected to the negative end of the voltage source while the other electrode is connected to the positive terminal. This negative terminal repels the free electrons in the semiconductor, which are being attracted to the positive end of the voltage source. The electron holes within the P-type material are repelled by the positive terminal and drawn across the depletion zone to the negative terminal. The charge moves across the diode as free electrons drop into holes and are boosted out again by the potential difference. If the diode is connected with the N-type material to the positive terminal and with the P-type material to the negative terminal, the charges are attracted to the terminals nearest to them, the depletion zone grows larger, and current does not flow across the diode.

The trick to getting diodes to emit light lies in the amount of energy released when free electrons fall into electron holes. Light consists of massless particles of energy called *photons*, and different amounts of energy produce different wavelengths—and colors—of light. Electrons travel in orbitals around the nucleus of an atom—the further away from the nucleus an electron's orbit is, the more energy it takes to maintain this orbit. Electrons generally travel through the outermost orbitals of an atom's electron shells as they move freely through a material. When free electrons in diodes drop into electron holes, they release energy as they enter an orbital closer to the atom's nucleus. The use of a different semiconductor material in a diode alters the energy gap between free electrons and electrons within holes and changes the amount of energy released and the color of light produced.

LEDs have many advantages over incandescent and fluorescent lights. They are brighter, consume less energy, and last longer. However, their expense makes them an impractical choice when it comes to lighting a room. Although early LEDs were usually used as indicator lights on electronics to show when they were on or off, they are now used in many different applications. Many traffic lights have recently been converted to much brighter LEDs to guarantee that the lights will have many more useful years than those of light bulbs. Automobile manufacturers have begun installing LEDs in new cars to improve the brightness of brake lights in an effort to make them more visible. LEDs now backlight some liquid-crystal-display screens; although the expense of manufacturing these types of large-screen televisions makes them uncommon, the displays of many smart phones incorporate them.

(continued from page 47)

Resistors are devices that electric circuits use to reduce the current by adding resistance. Coiling a thin wire with high resistance around a core creates a longer and narrower path, thus allowing resistors to provide greater resistance. Resistors come in many different amounts of resistance and are extremely commonplace in circuits today. Most resistors have color-coded outer shells to help identify the amount of resistance that they supply. The following table shows how to read the color codes on a resistor; the first two color bands show the first two numbers in the resistance, and the third color band shows the multiplier—what the first two numbers should be multiplied by to produce the actual resistance. These first three bands are evenly spaced with a wider gap between them and the fourth band to allow for easy identification. The fourth color band shows the resistor's tolerance—that is, to what degree the actual resistance can vary. Gold and silver bands—±5 percent and ±10 percent, respectively—are the most common, with smaller tolerances used for delicate circuits in which the resistance must be exactly right. Some resistors have a variable resistance in which the length of resistive material through which current must travel can be increased or decreased

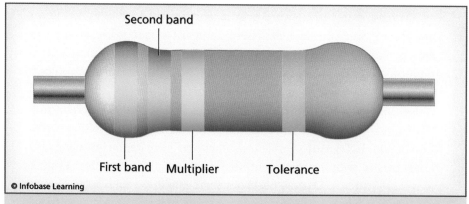

Second band

First band   Multiplier   Tolerance

© Infobase Learning

Using the color code in the table on page 51, the resistor shown above has a resistance of 27×10^5, or 2,700,000 ohms, with a tolerance of ±5%.

Four-Band Resistor Color Codes

COLOR	FIRST BAND (FIRST NUMBER)	SECOND BAND (SECOND NUMBER)	THIRD BAND (MULTIPLIER)	FOURTH BAND (TOLERANCE)
Black	0	0	10^0	
Brown	1	1	10^1	±1%
Red	2	2	10^2	±2%
Orange	3	3	10^3	
Yellow	4	4	10^4	
Green	5	5	10^5	±0.5%
Blue	6	6	10^6	±0.25%
Violet	7	7	10^7	±0.1%
Gray	8	8	10^8	±0.05%
White	9	9	10^9	
Gold			10^{-1}	±5%
Silver			10^{-2}	±10%

by turning a knob. These variable resistors are called *potentiometers* or *rheostats* and are commonly used in dimmer light switches and volume controls on radios.

A ground is occasionally part of an electric circuit and can be used to indicate a direct connection with the Earth or as a reference point from which other voltages are measured. A physical connection with the Earth serves to provide a path for the buildup of excess electrons caused by static electricity or to protect the circuit in case insulation fails and a dangerous voltage is produced. When measuring voltage, a change in potential difference is generally used; therefore, a reference point from which all measurements can be made is useful. The Earth makes a good reference point because it has a fairly constant potential difference. Another safety device commonly built into circuits is a **fuse**—an object with a small, thin filament that has a lower melting point than the rest of the electrical wiring. When the current gets too high, resistance causes the filament to heat and melt; this process opens the circuit and prevents the high current from reaching—and possibly damaging—other components.

One final type of possible component in a circuit takes measurements of the electricity traveling through the circuit or through specific parts of the circuit. A voltmeter measures the potential difference between two specific points on a circuit. A voltmeter must be hooked up in parallel—in a separate path—with a device so that its voltage can measured. An ammeter measures the current flowing through a circuit and must always be hooked up in series—within the same path—with a device so that it can measure the current flowing through the circuit. Multimeters are devices that can be used to measure voltage, current, or even resistance, although the meter must be set up correctly for each type of measurement.

CIRCUIT DIAGRAMS

When using words to describe a circuit, one must be extremely specific. It is not enough to say "three light bulbs connected to a battery" because that does not explain whether the light bulbs are in series or parallel to each other. In addition, everyone must understand the same language, which is not always the case when an electronic device may be designed in one country and assembled in another. A drawing of a circuit may be used; however, that requires some artistic ability and leaves some degree of uncertainty because not every person would draw each component the same way. For this reason, most engineers use circuit diagrams to quickly communicate the circuits that have been designed.

Circuit diagrams show a circuit in the simplest way possible with specific symbols used to represent the components within the circuit. Although circuit symbols have not been standardized,

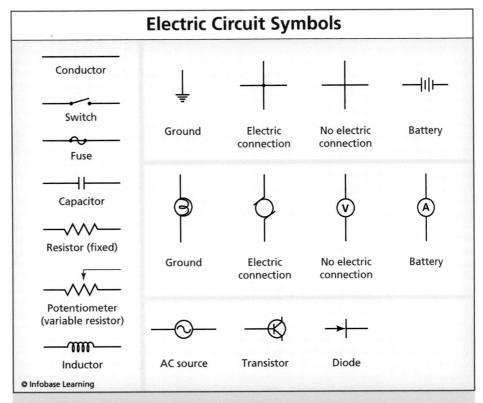

Electric Circuit Symbols

Conductor	Ground	Electric connection	No electric connection	Battery
Switch				
Fuse				
Capacitor	Ground	Electric connection	No electric connection	Battery
Resistor (fixed)				
Potentiometer (variable resistor)				
Inductor	AC source	Transistor	Diode	

© Infobase Learning

These symbols are some of the most commonly used circuit diagram symbols.

most symbols are the same worldwide and are easily recognized. Shown above are some of the circuit symbols that will be used in this book.

Two electrical wires that make a connection are shown with a dot at the connecting point to differentiate them from two insulating wires that cross with no connection. For the battery symbol, the end with the longer line represents the positive terminal, whereas the shorter line represents the negative—sometimes a positive and negative sign are shown to represent this. When using the symbol for a diode, the arrow must be pointing in the direction of conventional current to show the correct way to hook one up—with the cathode end connecting to the negative end of the voltage source.

When drawing a circuit diagram, one must follow the three steps listed below that make it easier to produce a consistent, easily read diagram. Circuit diagrams are drawn to be read left to right and top to bottom.

1. Draw the voltage source vertically at the far left. If the source is a battery, show the positive terminal at the top.
2. Draw the conductive path starting from the positive terminal—or the top of the voltage source. Make all lines straight and neat, making all turns in the wire precise angles, usually 90°.
3. Ensure that all components are shown in the proper order and with their correct symbols and that the circuit path continues until it reaches the negative terminal.

Care must be taken with the placement of some components because their function can depend on where they are located within a circuit. For example, a fuse must be placed in series with the components that it is designed to protect from too high of a current. A voltmeter must always be placed in parallel with a device so that it can measure the device's voltage, and an ammeter must be in series with a device so that it can measure the current flowing through the circuits. In order to be effective, switches must be in series with any device that they are designed to turn off; otherwise, when the current is stopped in one path, it can continue in another one.

CIRCUIT SAFETY

One of the most common dangers when dealing with electricity is a short circuit, which occurs when a path within the circuit has little or no resistance thereby delivering too much current. A short circuit can overheat and melt the wires, damage components within the circuit, or even cause a fire or an explosion.

Short circuits can occur when a new path is introduced within a circuit, such as a wire falling across a 9-volt battery and touching both terminals. Because the wire is so short, there is very little resistance, and the current becomes extremely high and causes the wire to become hot and the battery to possibly explode. Short circuits can also be caused by insulation wearing away in which two wires cross each other and make a connection where there should not be one.

Because many electrical fires in homes are caused by short circuits, several safety devices can be used in circuits to prevent the damage caused by overheating circuits. For example, one safety feature used in circuits is a fuse, designed to quickly melt when the current becomes too high and open the circuit. Fuses are cheap and easy to use, but they must be replaced every time that they melt, which is not always practical for everyday use. The circuits within buildings typically use a **circuit breaker** to prevent overheating. These circuit breakers act as a sort of reusable fuse whereby they open the circuit when the current becomes too high; however, once the current is lowered, the switch can be closed, and the breaker can be used again. One type of circuit breaker contains a strip of two different types of metals back to back. As current passes through the strip, the metal heats and grows hotter as the current becomes higher. All metals expand as they are heated, although different types of metals expand at different rates. When the current becomes too high, the strip becomes hotter, with one metal expanding more than the other, causing the strip to curl. The curling strip opens the switch and thus stops the flow of electrons and cools the circuit.

A **ground fault interrupter** is a safety device built into the power outlets in a building to protect against dangerous or fatal shocks. When a device is plugged into a power outlet, the outlet expects to receive the same current back as it sent out. A ground fault interrupter detects even very small changes in the current that goes out versus the current that returns and opens the circuit. Electrical current following a new path and traveling into the ground usually causes these changes. Outlets in bathroom and

Outlets in the kitchen and bathroom use ground fault interrupters as a safety feature to open the circuit when they detect small changes in current caused by extra paths, such as water. (Courtesy of Providence Electric)

kitchens must now have ground fault interrupters because of the proximity of water and its conductive abilities. If a woman curling her hair at the bathroom sink puts down the curling iron into a small puddle on the counter, any contact with that puddle could allow electrical current to flow through her body. A ground fault interrupter would quickly detect this change in the return current and open the switch, thus preventing serious injury to the woman.

SUMMARY

A circuit is a closed path that allows electrons to flow from a voltage source through components that use the electrical energy and then back to the source. The current flowing through circuits can either be direct current (DC) or alternating current (AC). Direct current exists when current flows in only one direction along the circuit, whereas alternating current exists when the current rapidly switches direction back and forth. Parts within a circuit can be connected in one of two ways: (1) they can be in series with each other—within the same path, or (2) they can be in parallel with each other—in a separate path.

Although there are many different devices that can be part of a circuit, all circuits must contain two things: (1) conductive wires to form a path and (2) a voltage source such as a battery or a generator. Capacitors can be included within circuits as a means to store and then release electrical energy. Circuits are typically designed to power some device such as a light bulb or an LED. Switches can be used to enable the circuit to be quickly opened or closed to stop or start the flow of electrons. A transistor is a device that changes the current that flows through it, typically making it larger. Resistors are used to add resistance to the circuit, slowing down the current to prevent overheating and damage to other components. A resistor typically uses color-coded bands on its surface to indicate the amount of resistance it provides. Grounds are used to provide safe removal of excess electrons into the Earth, thus preventing overheating of the circuit. Measurements are frequently taken within a circuit using a voltmeter to measure potential difference or an ammeter to measure current.

Circuit diagrams are a way to show exactly what devices are in a circuit and where they should be placed relative to each other. Special symbols are used to represent each type of device, and diagrams are meant to be read by anyone with a basic understanding of electronics. These diagrams help bridge the gap between electrical engineers who design circuits and the people who put them together and who may or may not speak the same language. When drawing circuit diagrams, one must be careful to place objects where they will be able to perform their task—for instance, voltmeters must be placed in parallel, ammeters must be placed in series, and fuses and switches must be placed in series with the objects that they need to turn on and off.

Because high amounts of electrical energy can be passed through an electric circuit, things can go wrong even under the best of conditions and become very dangerous. Short circuits— one of the most common causes of accidental house fires—are caused by electrical paths that are too short, thus providing little resistance and increasing the current to dangerous levels. Short circuits are created when new paths are added to a circuit, such as water connecting two wires or insulation being rubbed or eaten away. This excessive amount of current causes the wires to heat up, possibly causing fires and damaging other parts of the circuit. Two devices that protect against the effects of a short circuit are fuses and circuit breakers. Both of these devices cause the circuit to open when the current becomes too high—a fuse by melting and a circuit breaker by flipping a switch. Ground fault interrupters protect against shock when electrical current enters a person's body. These devices detect the small changes in current that indicate the presence of a new path—such as water or a person's body—and open the circuit.

Understanding electric circuits, their parts, and their dangers provides knowledge of modern electronic equipment. Electric circuits tie together previous knowledge about electricity, such as potential difference, electric field and forces, and current electricity. Chapter 5 specifically talks about the differences in voltage, current, and resistance in series and parallel circuits.

Series and Parallel Circuits

Chapter 5 investigates the two simplest types of circuits—series and parallel—and describes complex circuits that contain some components in series and others in parallel. The chapter also discusses each type of circuit individually, including an explanation on how current, voltage, and resistance are affected, depending on how the components are connected to each other. This chapter concludes the information on electricity by delving deeper into the types of circuits seen from day to day.

KIRCHHOFF'S CIRCUIT LAWS

In 1845, the German physicist Gustav Kirchhoff (1824–87) created two laws that help to explain the behavior of current and voltage in circuits through studying the work of Georg Ohm. These laws primarily describe the behavior of circuits in which the current does not vary. Kirchhoff's current law, or his first law, states that for any junction within a circuit, the current flowing into the junction is equal to the current flowing out. Electrical charge must be conserved as current flows through a circuit—no additional electrons or ions can be added or subtracted. When

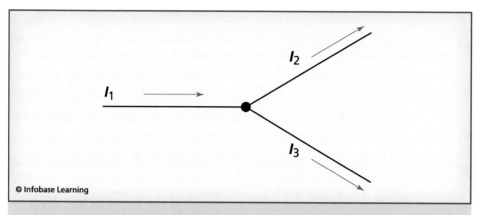

Kirchhoff's current law states that for this diagram, the incoming current, I_1, is equal to the sum of the outgoing currents, I_2 and I_3.

current approaches a split as shown in the figure above, the total current of the outgoing wires must be equal to the total incoming current.

Kirchhoff's voltage law, or his second law, states that for a closed circuit, the sum of the voltage in any one path must equal zero. This law assumes that the voltage supplied by the battery or other voltage source is positive, whereas the voltage used by each component—commonly called the *voltage drop*—is negative. Thus, the sum of the voltage used by all components in one path is equal to the voltage supplied by the battery. These laws explain why both current and voltage are calculated differently depending on the type of circuit.

SERIES CIRCUITS

Parts of a circuit are connected in series if they are within the same path of the circuit—the current must pass through one component to pass through the other. A circuit is a series circuit when all of its components are connected in series with each other, thus producing one path for electrons to flow through. In a series circuit, each device receives the same current because there is only one path for the current to flow, it must flow at the same rate everywhere. There are no junctions within a series circuit, so at no point does the current change. However, the voltage drop at each component within the circuit differs, depending on the resistance of that object. Kirchhoff's voltage law says that within one path—like a series circuit—the sum of the voltage drops for each component adds up to the total voltage delivered by the battery. Thus, the following equation can be used to calculate the voltage of the source or a specific component:

$$V_{source} = V_A + V_B + V_C + \dots$$

In this equation, V_A represents the voltage drop across the first component, V_B represents the second, and so on, adding as many

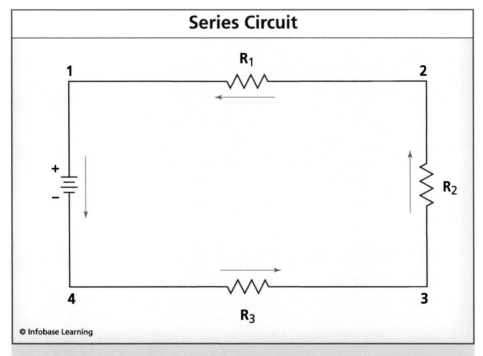

Series Circuit

© Infobase Learning

In a series circuit made of three different resistors, the current would be the same for each resistor, but the voltage for each will be different.

as needed. If the components all have the same resistance, their individual voltages will also be the same and will still sum to the total voltage supplied by the source.

The **equivalent resistance** of a circuit is the total resistance produced by all the components within the circuit. For a series circuit, the equivalent resistance can be found by summing the resistances supplied by each component, remembering that most components provide some resistance. The following equation can be used to calculate the equivalent resistance of a series circuit:

$$R_{eq} = R_A + R_B + R_C + \dots$$

Ohm's law can still be used to calculate the current, resistance, or voltage for either the circuit as a whole or for an individual component. However, care must be taken to use the voltage of the source only when using equivalent resistance and to use specific voltages and resistances when talking about a specific component.

The use of series circuits is limited on the basis that having one component stop functioning causes the entire circuit to stop working. For this reason, series circuits are impractical for large scale wiring, such as homes and buildings. Series circuits are more commonly used for small, internal circuits in electronics. One advantage for using a series circuit is that it uses less material for wiring and thus costs less. In addition, it provides a uniform current across the voltage, which can be necessary depending on the components.

PARALLEL CIRCUITS

In a parallel circuit, all components are connected in parallel to each other—in separate paths. One advantage to having multiple paths within a circuit is that the malfunction of one part has no effect on the other parts because the current does not have to go through one part in order to reach the other. According to Kirchhoff's current law, at each junction at which a new path is created, the incoming current must equal the outgoing current. Therefore, in a parallel circuit, the current is different in each path, and the sum of the currents in each path equals the total current for the entire circuit, as shown in the following equation:

$$I_{circuit} = I_A + I_B + I_C + \ldots$$

Kirchhoff's voltage law explains that the voltage provided by the source—in the example below, a battery—is equal to the voltage used by the components within a single path. This explanation means that, in the example below, each resistor has the same voltage—one that is equal to the voltage provided by the battery. In a parallel circuit, the equivalent resistance is calculated by tak-

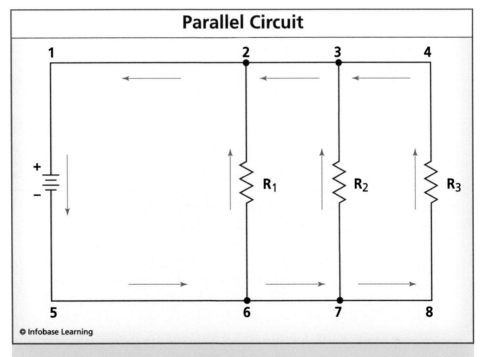

Parallel Circuit

© Infobase Learning

In a parallel circuit made of three different resistors, the voltage would be the same for each resistor, whereas the current would be different.

ing the reciprocal of the sum of the reciprocals of each resistor, as shown in the following equation:

$$\frac{1}{R_{eq}} = \frac{1}{R_A} + \frac{1}{R_B} + \frac{1}{R_C} + \ldots$$

The total resistance for the circuit is less than the resistance provided by each individual resistor. Ohm's law can also be used with parallel circuits to calculate current, resistance, and voltage for the entire circuit or for each individual path of the circuit.

Parallel circuits are more frequently encountered than series circuits because their ability to have one component malfunction while another continues to work makes them more practical for general use. Parallel circuits also deliver the same maximum voltage to every component, allowing, for example, brighter lights and louder noises. Adding a resistor in parallel to a circuit lowers the equivalent resistance because the total resistance for a parallel circuit is always less than the resistance of the individual resistors.

COMPLEX CIRCUITS

Many more complex circuits have some parts that are in series with each other and other parts that are parallel to each other. Although these circuits share the benefits of both series and parallel circuits, calculating current, resistance, and voltage becomes more difficult. No one rule can be applied for the entirety of a complex circuit; instead, the circuit must be broken down and simplified by looking at parts of the circuit that are in series or are in parallel. For example, Resistors 2 and 3 in the circuit shown on page 65 are connected in parallel to each other. Finding the equivalent resistance for this circuit requires a calculation of the total resistance of these two resistors in parallel to each other. Then, because Resistor 1 is in series with both Resistors 2 and 3, the circuit can be redrawn to show one resistor with resistance equal to the equivalent resistance of Resistors 2 and 3. What remains is a series circuit with two resistors, which makes the final equivalent resistance simple to find.

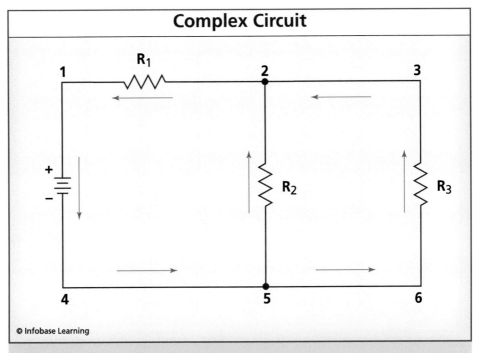

Complex Circuit

R₁

1   R₁   2   3

+ −

R₂   R₃

4   5   6

© Infobase Learning

In this complex circuit, Resistors 1 and 2 and Resistors 1 and 3 are in series with each other, whereas Resistors 2 and 3 are connected parallel to each other.

Complex circuits are most commonly used for large-scale wiring, such as in homes or in cars. Wiring in modern homes involves several different circuits, each with a circuit breaker in series with the entire circuit so that when the circuit breaker switches the circuit off to prevent overheating, the entire circuit turns off. For this reason, setting off a circuit breaker turns off multiple outlets and lights within an area of a house. However, the components within each circuit are connected in parallel to each other so that one light bulb burning out does not turn off the entire circuit. Manufacturers wire cars with complex circuits set up in much the same way, but they use fuses instead of circuit breakers to prevent overheating caused by too much current. These setups allow for

(continues on page 68)

Christmas Lights

Christmas lights are a good example of the benefits and problems that arise from circuits being connected in series or in parallel. The first Christmas lights were small 5- or 10-watt bulbs—similar to those used in nightlights—strung together. The disadvantages to these early strands were that they consumed a lot of electricity, were expensive, and produced a lot of heat that made them dangerous to leave on for long periods of time on a tree. One benefit to these lights was that they were connected in parallel to provide the same voltage to each bulb, which meant that if one light went out, the entire strand did not go dark. In the 1970s, modern Christmas lights equipped with the 2.5-volt miniature lights were introduced, providing a cheaper, safer, and less energy-consuming way to decorate for the holidays through wiring the circuit in series. Unfortunately, these miniature lights do have one downside when it comes to ease of use. Most people have experienced the annoyance that comes when one light burns out in a strand of Christmas lights and the entire strand—or a section—turns off, requiring a search through each light until the culprit is located.

These early strands consisted of 48 to 50 of these 2.5-volt miniature lights connected in series so that the entire strand required about 120 volts from its voltage source, typically a wall outlet providing exactly that amount of voltage. Longer strands are created by wiring several of these 50-bulb strands in parallel to each other, providing each strand with the same 120 volts. In recent years, these miniature lights have been made with a shunt wire in place below the filament that allows current to continue to flow through the wires of the bulb—without producing any light—even when the filament eventually melts. This configuration allows the other lights in the same series strand with the bulb to stay lit and provides easy identification of the light that needs to be replaced. However, removing the bulb still causes the entire strand to go out.

In order to make a strand of Christmas lights blink, a blinker miniature light can be added at any place along the strand. A blinker light contains an extra piece of metal near the filament called a bimetallic strip that bends when the metal gets hot and then straightens as it cools. When the light turns on, the

Many Christmas tree lights use multiple wires to place the lights in parallel so that one light can go out without turning off all the lights. (Courtesy of Greatoccasions.com)

filament quickly becomes hot, causing the strip to bend and breaking the electric connection. This process turns off the blinker light and every other light within the same series strand. Once the current stops flowing, the filament rapidly cools, and the strip straightens back out making the connection again and allowing current to flow; the cycle is repeated over and over. Newer and more expensive blinking lights can use an electronic controller to cause the lights to blink in a specific pattern, such as in time to a song.

(continued from page 65)
each component within the circuit to receive the same amount of voltage so that all outlets in American homes will provide the same 120 volts.

SUMMARY

In 1845, Gustav Kirchhoff wrote two laws based on research done by Georg Ohm, which described how the voltage, current, and resistance of a circuit were changed depending on its design. Kirchhoff's current law states that the current that goes into a junction is equal to the current that comes out. For example, if a wire splits into two paths, the sum of the current in those two paths is equal to the original current before the split. Kirchhoff's voltage law states that the sum of the voltage used by the components within a single path of a circuit is equal to the voltage provided by the voltage source. These laws have been instrumental in helping scientists understand the behavior of series and parallel circuits.

In a series circuit—in which all parts are connected in one path—the current is the same throughout that path. However, in accordance with Kirchhoff's voltage law, the voltage for different components changes depending on their resistance, and the sum of all these voltages is equal to the voltage provided by the source. The equivalent resistance of the circuit is equal to the sum of the resistance of each component within the circuit. Series circuits have the advantage of providing a uniform current, but they do not provide maximum voltage to each component. Adding new parts to the circuit only decreases the voltage that each part receives from the battery. Another problem with this type of circuit is that when any part of the circuit stops working, the current stops flowing completely, turning off the entire circuit.

Parallel circuits provide multiple paths through which current can flow; this configuration allows parts of the circuit to be off while others are still on. In a parallel circuit, the voltage is the same within every path, although the current fluctuates from one component to the next. The sum of the current passing through each component is equal to the total current of the circuit, which is dependent on the voltage provided and the equivalent resistance. For a parallel circuit, equivalent resistance is calculated by summing the reciprocals of the resistance for each device and then by taking the reciprocal of that value. Parallel circuits have the advantage of providing the maximum voltage for each component within the circuit.

Many circuits have portions in series with each other, and other parts are connected in parallel; this configuration provides the benefits of both types of circuits. In order to calculate current, resistance, or voltage for this type of circuit, each portion must be looked at in separate pieces. For example, find the equivalent resistance for a portion of the circuit that is connected in parallel and then look at what that portion is in series with. Complex circuits are frequently used when large circuits must be created, such as in homes and cars. Although the circuits in a home are largely designed in parallel, so that one light can be off while another light is on, the circuit breakers that prevent overheating must be placed in series with the entire circuit to effectively protect the circuit.

This chapter completes the discussion about electricity alone, from static electricity to current electricity. The next chapters discuss magnetism and its relationship with electricity. This relationship is one of the four fundamental forces that drive many of the interactions between matter in the world, including some of those most commonly used technology.

6

Magnetism

Chapter 6 begins by describing the types of magnets, how they are made, and their properties, particularly magnetic fields. The chapter then discusses the link between electricity and magnetism illustrated with the discovery of electromagnetism. The chapter continues with a discussion of three right-hand rules used to describe the results of electromagnetism, including when and how to use each rule. Finally, the chapter details the uses of electromagnetism in everyday items, such as doorbells and speakers.

PROPERTIES OF MAGNETS

Although people may not always be aware of the many ways in which magnets are used, these devices have become rather commonplace in our modern world. They are placed on refrigerators to secure paper or clippings, under cars to hold extra keys, and in the speakers of our cell phones. Despite their ubiquitous nature, few people understand why some materials are magnetic, whereas others are not. Items that can be magnetized in such a way to produce a detectable amount of magnetism are called *ferromagnetic* or *ferrimagnetic*. These materials include metals, such as iron, nickel,

Lodestones are natural, permanent magnets. (Courtesy of Wikimedia)

and cobalt, along with some mixtures of rare earth metals. Some minerals can also be magnetized, such as lodestones that are naturally magnetic. Ferromagnetic and ferrimagnetic materials can be classified as either hard or soft. Hard magnetic materials are those that are difficult to make magnetic but that keep their magnetism for a long time, whereas soft materials magnetize easily but also lose their magnetism without difficulty.

Magnets can be either temporary magnets or permanent magnets, depending on the duration of their magnetism. A temporary magnet is magnetic only while it is in contact with another magnet. Once removed from this other magnet, a temporary magnet loses its induced magnetism. A temporary magnet can also be made by rubbing it with another permanent magnet, which causes it to briefly retain its magnetism. A permanent magnet can be produced by being near or in contact with another magnet or by being rubbed with another magnet; however, these materials do not lose their magnetism.

Every magnet possesses two poles—a north pole and a south pole. Cutting a magnet in half never produces a magnet with only one pole; it just makes a smaller magnet with both a north and south pole. Similar to the attraction and repulsion of electric charges, with magnets, opposite poles attract, whereas like poles repel each other. The north pole of a magnet is called such because it is the end of the magnet that is attracted to the geographic north pole of the Earth, which is actually the magnetic south pole. Both poles of a magnet will attract a ferromagnetic material because it can be temporarily magnetized. A **magnetic field** is the area around a magnet in which these attractive and repulsive forces are felt. Magnetic field lines can be drawn to show the strength of a magnetic field around a magnet, or the magnetic field can be shown by scattering metal fillings over a magnet, as shown in the picture to the left. Magnetic field lines are closest together at the poles—showing that the field is the strongest in these areas—and furthest apart in the center of the magnet. These lines travel from the north pole to the south pole of the magnet, passing through the magnet in an unbroken loop.

Iron fillings can be used to show the magnetic field lines around a magnet. (Courtesy of the Center for Computational Heliophysics in Hawaii, Center for Astronomy)

Earth's Changing Magnetic Field

Many 20th-century scientists who studied the rock around mid-ocean ridges discovered at a certain point—indicating a specific time period—that the magnetism of the rocks were opposite of what was expected. This discovery led to the realization that the Earth's magnetic field has flipped, many times in fact. Although the frequency of this magnetic reversal is erratic, the most recent reversal occurred about 780,000 years ago. Scientists believe that changes that occur within the molten outer core of iron near the center of the Earth cause this reversal.

The effects of one of these reversals are not completely known because humans were not around the last time one occurred. All compasses would certainly end up pointing to the geographic south pole, and all navigational equipment using the magnetic field would malfunction. Birds and other animals that migrate would likely become confused and unable to find their orientation, possibly resulting in loss of life. Some scientists theorize that past magnetic reversals occurred around the same time as mass extinctions of animals. If the field weakens or disappears during this process, it may allow dangerous cosmic radiation typically deflected by the magnetic field to reach the Earth's surface, which could be catastrophic. Thankfully, mathematical models show that the field will likely not disappear altogether during the reversal and will instead have north and south poles in random and changing locations. Life on Earth has evolved through these reversals in the past and is hopefully equipped to survive the next one, whenever that may occur.

Metals are the most common ferromagnetic material because they have many unpaired electrons in the orbitals of their atoms. All of these unpaired electrons spin in the same way, creating tiny magnets that all travel in the same direction. When many atoms together have all their unpaired electrons spinning parallel to each other, a **domain** is created. All of the tiny magnets within

Iron's Magnetism

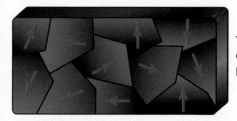

The atoms in iron line up within regions called *domains*. The different domains point in many different directions.

When iron is magnetized, the domains point in the same direction.

© Infobase Learning

This diagram shows how the domains within a piece of iron originally cancel each other out; however, after they are magnetized, they line up to produce a magnetic field.

a domain are lined up, creating a relatively strong magnetic field. Domains are extremely small, and even a small piece of ferromagnetic metal will contain a huge number of them. It requires the least amount of energy for these domains to be randomly scattered, each magnetic field cancelling out another, leaving little or no net magnetic field. When these types of materials are placed within a magnetic field, the domains all line up with the field and reinforce each other to produce an overall magnetic field. When removed from the outside magnetic field, the domains remain lined up to produce a permanent magnet. In a temporary magnet the domains return to their randomized positions, and the material quickly loses its magnetism.

ELECTROMAGNETISM

The four fundamental forces of nature are the gravitational force, electromagnetic force, weak nuclear force, and strong nuclear force. The electromagnetic force produces both electricity and magnetism and their interactions with each other. However, before the 19th century, scientists believed that electricity and magnetism were entirely separate. In 1820, the Danish physicist Hans Christian Ørsted (1777–1851) was giving a lecture on electricity and magnetism. During the lecture, he insisted that electricity and magnetism must be related and that one could be converted into the other. He based his lecture entirely on his philosophy that all forces ultimately arise from the same source. While lecturing, Ørsted placed a compass near to a current carrying wire, hopeful of the results, and was rewarded when the compass deflected and showed a magnetic field perpendicular to the wire. Further research showed that an electric current passing through a wire creates a magnetic field in a circle around the wire; this research opened up the field of electromagnetism.

The magnetic field produced by a single, straight wire is relatively weak; however, wrapping the wire into coils produces multiple magnetic fields in the same direction that strengthen each other, thus creating a stronger magnetic field. These coils of wire produce an **electromagnet**—a temporary magnet formed by electricity—sometimes also called a *solenoid*. Electromagnets have a north and a south pole and can be strengthened by adding more coils of wire or by placing a ferromagnetic core within the coil. Modern technology uses

Hans Christian Ørsted discovered electromagnetism in 1820. (Courtesy of the Dibner Library of the History and Science of Technology)

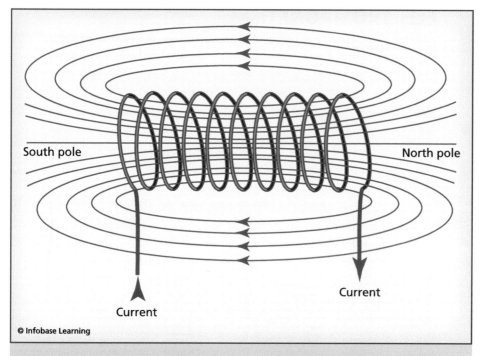

South pole

North pole

Current

Current

© Infobase Learning

An electromagnet can be created by coiling a current-carrying wire so that the magnetic fields produced by each portion of the wire reinforce each other.

electromagnets to a great extent because their magnetic properties can be instantly turned off and on by stopping and starting the flow of electricity.

If a current-carrying wire is placed within a magnetic field, the wire will experience a force pushing it in a direction perpendicular to the magnetic field. This process is caused by the induced magnetic field generated by the interaction of the current-carrying wire with the magnetic field that is already in place in either an attractive or repulsive manner. The following equation calculates the magnitude of this force:

$$F = BIL$$

In this equation, F represents the force measured in newtons (N), B is a measurement of the strength of the magnetic field measured in teslas (T), I is the current measured in amps (A), and L is a measurement of the length of the current-carrying wire measured in meters (m). Thus, a stronger current, more powerful magnets, or a longer wire all help to increase the force exerted on the wire when it is placed in a magnetic field.

Because each spinning electron produces a tiny magnetic field, electrons do not have to be moving through a wire to be affected by a magnetic field. Any charged particle experiences a force when moving through a magnetic field, unless it is moving parallel to the direction of the field. This force is used by cathode-ray tube televisions when magnets manipulate the electron beams, directing them to the correct pixels to produce an image. This force is directly proportional to the strength of the magnetic field, the magnitude of the charge, the velocity of the charge, and the angle between the magnetic field and the direction that the particle is traveling. When the charged particle is moving perpendicular to the magnetic field—when the force is at its maximum—the force can be calculated with the following equation,

$$F = Bqv$$

where q measures the charge on the particle in coulombs (C), and v measures the velocity of the particle in meters per second (m/s). When the motion of the charged particle is not perpendicular to the magnetic field, only the portion of the velocity in the perpendicular direction is used in the above equation.

RIGHT-HAND RULES

In the late 1800s, John Ambrose Fleming (1849–1945), an English professor of electrical technology, invented the right-hand rule as a way to determine the direction of a vector product in situations where three vectors must be at right angles to each other. The right-hand rule is most commonly used in electromagnetism and has been developed into three distinct uses, or rules. It is important to remember that when this rule is applied to electromagnetism, the right-hand rule assumes the flow of positive charge—conventional current.

The **first right-hand rule** is used to determine the direction of the magnetic field around a current-carrying wire or the direction of the current when the field is known. If a wire is held in the right hand with the thumb pointing in the direction of conventional current, the magnetic field is in the direction that the fingers wrap around the wire. This use of the right-hand rule is a different form in which one of the vectors is rotating around the other. The left hand can be used to find the direction of the magnetic field with charge current.

Solenoids are an important part of electromagnetism; accordingly, the **second right-hand rule** is used to locate the north pole of an electromagnet. This rule shows the relationship between the direction of conventional current through the coils of the solenoid and the north pole of the produced magnet. If a solenoid is held in the right hand with the fingers curling in the direction of conventional current through the coils, the thumb points in the direction of the north pole. To find the north pole for charge current, the same rules are used with the left hand. According to the figure on page 76, holding the coil in the right hand with the fingers wrapping around the coil in the direction of conventional current—into and then out of the page—the north pole of the electromagnet is on the far right of the solenoid.

The two equations in the previous section allow for the calculation of the magnitude of the force on a current-carrying wire or a charged particle, and the **third right-hand rule** allows for a determination of the direction. When the right hand is held flat, with the fingers pointing in the direction of the magnetic field—flowing from north to south poles—and the thumb is pointing in the direction of conventional current or in the direction of the velocity of a positive particle, the palm of the hand points in the direction of the force on the wire or particle. This rule can be applied to charge current or with a negative particle when the left hand is used instead of the right hand.

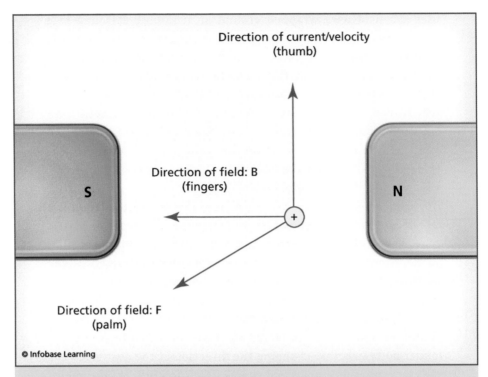

Direction of current/velocity
(thumb)

Direction of field: B
(fingers)

S

N

+

Direction of field: F
(palm)

© Infobase Learning

The third right-hand rule shows that with a magnetic field traveling right to left and a particle moving upward, the force on the particle is outward from the page.

USING ELECTROMAGNETISM

The fact that electrical current running through a wire produces a magnetic field is applied in many different forms presently, although this chapter will only discuss a few of these applications. One of the earliest uses of electromagnetism to perform a task was the galvanometer. The German physicist Johann Schweigger (1779–1857) is credited with creating the first galvanometer in fall 1820—later in same year that Ørsted discovered the magnetic field produced by current. The galvanometer was named in honor of Luigi Galvani, the physicist who discovered that touching metal to a frog's leg made it twitch. The simplest type of galvanometer uses a coil of wire wrapped around an iron core attached to a spring. As current flows through the wire it produces a magnetic field that causes the core to rotate because of the attractive and repulsive forces between the magnetic field produced and that of the permanent magnets that surround it. As the amount of current is increased, the electromagnet and resulting magnetic field are strengthened and therefore cause the coil to deflect more and send the needle farther along on the scale. The galvanometer enabled Georg Ohm to make quantitative measurements of current, which led to the development of Ohm's law.

Inside every speaker is a permanent magnet that surrounds a coil of wire that is wrapped around the base of a paper or plastic cone. When electrical current flows through the coil, it becomes an electromagnet, which is either repelled by, or attracted to, the permanent magnet, depending on the orientation of its poles. This force causes the cone to either be pushed forward or pulled back, creating sound waves through the compression of air molecules. Higher current causes the force to be stronger and to produce a louder noise, whereas changing the direction of the current swaps the electromagnet's poles and changes the direction of movement. The pattern of the waves produced determines the frequency and pitch of the sound emitted.

The motor is probably the most widely used piece of machinery that uses electromagnetism. The motor is used in cars, it is used to run the fans in computers, and it is used any time electrical energy is converted into mechanical energy. A simple direct current motor, like the one shown on page 81, consists of a voltage source, a commutator (a device that periodically reverses the current direction between the rotor and the external circuit), a coil of wire called an *armature*, and permanent magnets. As current flows from the voltage source—typically a battery—through the armature, the wire is attracted and repulsed by the permanent magnets until it completes half of a turn. At this point, the commutator allows the current to change direction, which causes the attractive and repulsive forces to continue until the circuit is completed—at which point, the process starts over. Attaching the

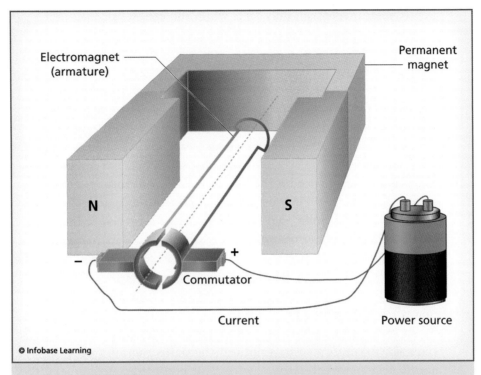

A simple direct current motor uses electrical energy to produce mechanical energy. Attaching a drive shaft to the loop of this motor allows that mechanical energy to be used for some purpose.

armature to a drive shaft allows the mechanical energy to be used to turn wheels, a fan, or any number of other items.

SUMMARY

When a material is able be magnetic strongly enough to affect objects around it or when an object is attracted to a magnet, that material is said to be ferromagnetic or ferrimagnetic. These materials are typically metals, alloys of metals, or minerals—like the naturally magnetic lodestone. Some of these materials become magnets simply by being in contact with, or near, another magnet. If their magnetism only lasts while the contact persists, the magnet is a temporary magnet. If the material remains magnetic even after the original magnet is removed, a permanent magnet has been produced.

Every magnet has two poles—a north pole and a south pole—that are as far from each other as possible and that are named according to which of the Earth's geographic poles they seek. The opposite poles of two magnets attract each other, whereas the same poles repel. The area in which this attractive and repulsive force can be experienced is the magnetic field. The magnetic field around a magnet travels from the north pole to the south pole, is strongest at these poles, and is weakest in the center of the magnet. The huge number of regions in which all the unpaired electrons spin the same direction that exists within every magnetic material creates a magnetic field. When these regions—called *domains*—all line up with each other instead of randomizing and cancelling each other out, a magnet is produced.

In spring 1820, the field of electromagnetism was born when Hans Christian Ørsted first noticed the deflection of a compass needle near a current-carrying wire. This proof that current passing through a wire produces a magnetic field in a circular pattern around that wire was monumental. It was soon discovered that coiling the wire produced a stronger field by creating an electromagnet, which could be made even stronger by adding more coils, adding a metal core, or increasing the voltage passing through the coil. When a current-carrying wire or a moving charged particle is placed in a magnetic field, the wire or particle experiences a force on it because of the interaction between its induced magnetic field and the original field.

Right-hand rules are a convenient way to determine the direction of magnetic fields or forces in a three-dimensional space. The first rule allows one to determine the direction of a magnetic field around a straight current-carrying wire by the visualization of holding the wire in the right hand with the thumb pointing in the direction of conventional current. Now the fingers are curled around the wire in the same direction as the magnetic field. The second rule is used when the wire is coiled to create an electromagnet to determine the location of that magnet's north pole. If the coil is held in the right hand with the fingers curling around the coil in the direction that conventional current travels, the thumb is pointing to the electromagnet's north pole. The third and final right-hand rule finds the direction of the force on a positively charged particle or current-carrying wire in a magnetic field. When holding the right hand flat with the fingers pointing in the direction of the magnetic field and the thumb pointing in the direction of the current in the wire or the particle's velocity, the palm of the hand shows the direction of the force.

This force between the magnetic field of an electromagnet and the field surrounding a permanent magnet is used in many different types of machines. The galvanometer, an early ammeter, uses this force to measure the current traveling through a wire. Speakers use the force to push a paper or plastic cone back and forth, thus compressing air molecules and producing sound waves. Motors are used in any machine that needs to convert electrical energy into mechanical energy, such as a car or a fan. One important aspect of a motor is that the current flowing through the electromagnet must change direction regularly to keep it spinning.

Although the fact that electrical current produces a magnetic field is a large piece of electromagnetism, it is not the entire picture. Ørsted was certain that electrical current could produce magnetism because they were, in fact, the same force. In that case, the opposite should also be true; magnetism should be able to produce electricity. The final chapter covers this last piece of electromagnetism—electromagnetic induction.

7

Electromagnetic Induction

Chapter 7 completes the discussion of electromagnetism by explaining electromagnetic induction from how it was discovered to how it is used today. The chapter explains the electromotive force (EMF) that arises from electromagnetic induction and describes its uses. The final section of the chapter explains mutual inductance and how it is used in transformers, particularly for use in large-scale power grids.

DISCOVERING ELECTROMAGNETIC INDUCTION

Despite now having two electrical units named in honor of him—farads measuring capacitance and faraday measuring charge—the British scientist Michael Faraday (1791–1867) was originally more interested in chemistry and metallurgy than electricity and magnetism. Faraday only began his studies in this field in 1821—the year after Ørsted's discovery of the magnetic field produced around a current-carrying wire—when a friend requested he write a history of the study of electricity and magnetism. Despite receiving little formal education and being unable to perform higher math such as calculus, Faraday greatly influenced scientific discovery mostly because he strove to always provide experimental support for an idea. While reviewing the research on electricity and magnetism Faraday, became convinced that if flowing electricity produces a magnetic field, then magnetism must also produce electricity. It took him 10 years to find the connection and to prove his belief, which later came to be called **electromagnetic induction**.

During this time, Faraday conducted several experiments in an attempt to prove that magnetism can create electricity, but he was unsuccessful. He also continued to work in other fields, including optics and acoustics. Finally in fall 1831, Faraday conducted the experiment shown on page 86(a). He found that turning the current through coil X off and on—by way of the switch—caused the galvanometer to read a changing current through coil Y. Through this experiment, Faraday proved the existence of electromagnetic induction. The current flowing through coil X produced a magnetic field within the iron ring, and as opening and closing the switch changed the current, it also changed the magnetic field, which then induced a current to flow through coil Y. At almost the same time, American teacher Joseph Henry (1797–1878) also discovered electromagnetic induction, but he did not publish his work until after Michael Faraday, leaving Faraday to get most of the credit.

Faraday's further experiments showed that any changing magnetic field could induce current to flow, and the easiest way to cause the magnetic field to change was to have relative motion between the magnet and the wire, either by moving the wire, moving the magnet, or moving both in different ways. The fact that the magnetic field must be changing was the key that had prevented him from proving the existence of electromagnetic induction for 10 years. Eventually, Faraday used his deductions about electromagnetism to create a dynamo, an early version of a generator used to convert mechanical energy into electrical energy. Although not all of the scientific community originally accepted the link between electricity and magnetism, it became widely ac-

Faraday's Experiments on Electromagnetism

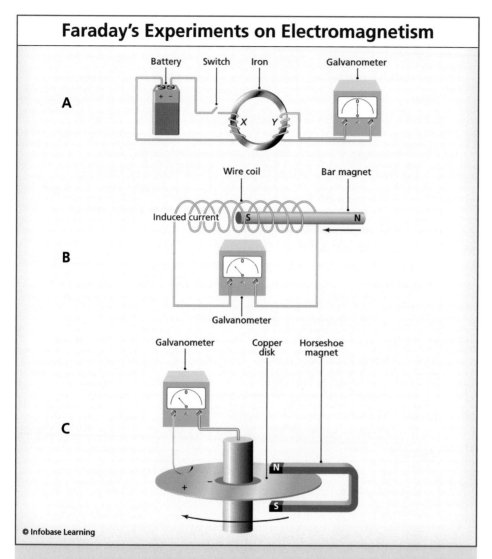

© Infobase Learning

(a) In an experiment like this one, Faraday first discovered electromagnetic induction. The changing current flowing through one coil induces current in the second coil. (b) Further experiments allowed Faraday to see that the magnet and the wire need to be in motion relative to each other. (c) Faraday's experiments led him to develop the dynamo, the precursor to the generator.

cepted after the 1873 publication of four equations by the Scottish mathematician James Clerk Maxwell (1831–79) that provide a mathematical basis for electromagnetism.

ELECTROMOTIVE FORCE

The term **electromotive force** *(EMF)* can be used to describe the potential difference given to charges by a battery or by a changing magnetic field. For the purposes of this book, this term will be used to mean the same thing as electric potential difference and voltage, although in other situations the phrase is used to mean something slightly different or more specific, such as only the voltage produced through electromagnetic induction. EMF is another term from before electricity was well understood because it does not describe a force at all; instead, it is the energy per unit charge available to move those charges.

When a wire is moved through a magnetic field, work is done to move the charges, and in accordance with the work-energy theorem, the amount of work done is equal to the charge in energy. This work causes the charges' electric potential energy to increase, and this change causes an electric potential difference, or EMF. The amount of voltage produced depends on the strength of the magnetic field (B), the length of the wire being moved (L), and the relative velocity between the wire and the magnet (v).

$$EMF = BLv$$

The following equation shows this relationship:
Care must be taken when using the above equation to ensure that velocity (v) is used and not voltage (V). EMF is measured in the same units as voltage and potential difference—volts.

USING INDUCED EMF

EMF, or voltage, induced through a changing magnetic field can be used in several different ways, like shake or magnetic flashlights. These flashlights never need a battery and can be easily recharged

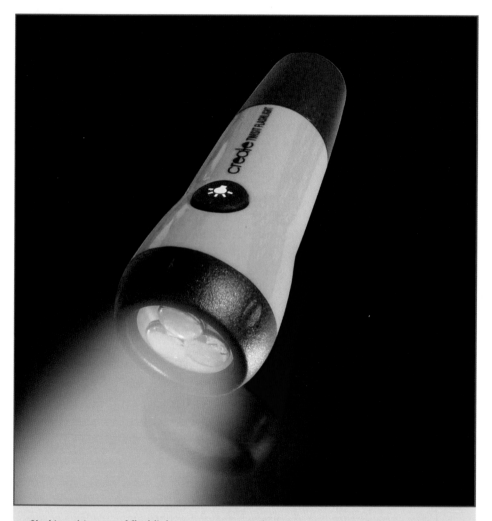

Shaking this type of flashlight generates enough current to produce light through electromagnetic induction. (Courtesy of Bestb2b.com)

with just 30 to 60 seconds of shaking. Shaking these flashlights causes a magnet to pass through a coil of wire, creating a current. A capacitor stores the current, delivering it to the light slowly over time when the "on" button is pressed. The stronger the magnet used, the quicker the charge is generated. The size of the capacitor determines how much charge can be stored, but some of these flashlights can produce light for up to 20 minutes after charging.

Microphones are the opposite of speakers in both what they do and how they do it. Speakers produce sound from an electrical current, and microphones create an electrical current from a sound wave. A speaker uses the magnetic field produced by electrical current to move a voice cone, which produces sound waves. In some types of microphones, sound waves move a thin plastic or metal diaphragm with a coil of wire attached in and out of a magnetic field, producing an electrical current in the wire. In fact, some speakers can be rewired in such a manner to allow their voice cones act as diaphragms, and they can be used as microphones.

Generators are devices that convert mechanical energy into electrical energy through the process of electromagnetic induction. In some cars' generators, are attached to the same drive shaft turned by the mechanical energy produced by the motor. For the generator, this drive shaft turns the armature within a magnetic field, inducing a current to flow through the armature and back to the car battery or to some other source. Portable generators are often used to power important equipment in hospitals and homes when the electrical energy flowing into the house is cut off as a result of downed power lines. Most power plants use generators to convert mechanical energy into the electrical energy used in homes and businesses. This mechanical energy can come in many forms, such as water, wind, or steam—from coal burning plants—turning turbines.

As the armature of a generator turns through a magnetic field, the current produced varies in both strength and direction. The third right-hand rule can be used to find the direction of the current produced, and it shows that when the coil spins in the same direction, the current reverses every half spin. The strength varies because the coil is not always moving through the same strength magnetic field or the same number of magnetic field lines. When the coil or armature is closest to the poles of the magnets, the current produced is the greatest because the magnetic field is at

its strongest in those locations. When the coil is equidistance between the two poles, the current is at its lowest because the magnetic field is weakest there.

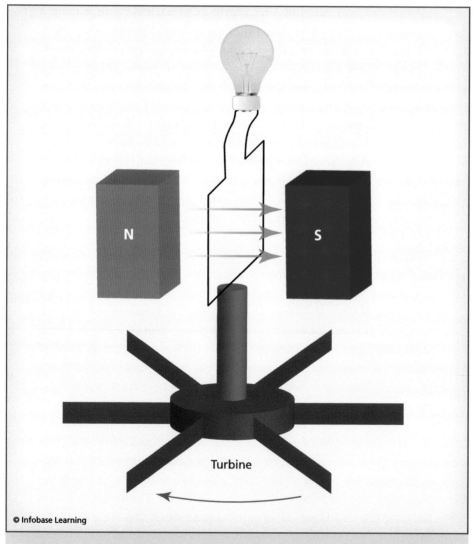

This generator converts the mechanical energy that turns the turbine into electrical energy to light the light bulb.

Generators versus Alternators

Generators and alternators are each devices that turn mechanical energy into electrical energy; the difference between them lies in the type of current produced. An *alternator* is any generator that produces alternating current (AC), although the term is almost exclusively used to refer to the AC generators used in conjunction with cars and other internal combustion engines. Before the 1960s, cars came with direct current (DC) generators, which seemed effective because the items using the current required DC. However, the armature in any generator produces current that changes direction every half turn as a result of the changing of the magnetic field around it. In order for a generator to provide DC, a commutator—a device with a series of different electrical contacts—is attached to the armature spinning within the magnetic field. Metal brushes touch different contacts as the armature spins in such a way as to keep the outgoing polarity the same at all times.

An alternator is constructed slightly differently. The armature in an alternator is stationary, and the magnets are spinning within it, thus allowing for direct electrical connection with the armature instead of through brushes as in a generator. As magnets have gotten both smaller and stronger, alternators have become cheaper to manufacture. This design also allows the magnets to spin faster than the armature of generators could, producing a higher current in a shorter amount of time. Diodes within the alternator change the produced AC into the necessary DC.

The advantages to using an alternator quickly caused it to completely replace generators in car engines, despite the need to change the current produced. Although generators are around 60 percent efficient—losing 40 percent of the mechanical energy to things like friction—alternators are closer to 90 percent efficient. Alternators are also significantly sturdier; they have less moving parts and have done away with brushes entirely because the brushes sliding along the armature lost energy to heat and sparks. In addition, alternators are cheaper to produce and lighter weight than generators are, making them the obvious choice in new car construction.

The current delivered by a generator constantly fluctuates between the maximum current possible—in either direction—and zero, and as the current oscillates, so does the voltage. Describing the effective current and effective voltage delivered by a generator instead of the maximum values is common practice because this description gives a better idea of the actual values over time. The following equations provide a simple way to calculate the effective values from the maximum values:

$$I_{eff} = 0.707 * I_{Max}$$
$$V_{eff} = 0.707 * V_{Max}$$

LENZ'S LAW

In 1833, the Russian physicist Heinrich Lenz (1804–65) proposed that an induced current is always oriented to oppose the change or motion that caused it, which later became known as Lenz's law. When an EMF is generated within a wire as a result of a changing magnetic field, the induced current in the wire produces a new magnetic field that opposes the change that produced it, thus attempting to keep the magnetic field constant. In generators, this opposing magnetic field applies a force that resists the motion of the armature—the larger the current produced, the larger the opposing force. Some of the mechanical energy put into the generator is lost in overcoming this force instead of being converted into electrical energy. Lenz's law also affects motors because the magnetic field created by the current-carrying wire induces a current to flow in the opposite direction within the wire. The potential difference that causes this opposing current to flow is sometimes called back-EMF. The result of Lenz's law in motors is such that some current is always lost as a result of being negated by the opposing current.

MUTUAL INDUCTANCE

When a current flows through a solenoid, a magnetic field is produced, and when that current is changing—like AC—then the magnetic field is also changing. If a second solenoid is within this changing magnetic field, a new current will be induced in this solenoid in a process called **mutual inductance**. In accordance with Lenz's law, the new current is in such a direction as to produce a magnetic field that opposes the changes of the original field. Mutual inductance is strengthened when the two solenoids share one core, particularly if that core is ferromagnetic. Transformers use the principle of mutual inductance to produce a new electrical current with more or less voltage than the original current.

Transformers like these lower the voltage of the electricity sent out from the power plant in order to be usable in homes. (Courtesy of Wikimedia)

The voltage of the current induced in the second coil is proportional to the number of coils in the second coil. Thus, going from more to less coils causes a decrease in the resulting voltage and is called a *step-down transformer*. When the number of coils increases, the voltage increases as well, creating a *step-up transformer*. The following equation shows the relationships between the number of coils, voltage, and current in the primary and secondary coils of an ideal transformer:

$$\frac{N_p}{N_s} = \frac{V_p}{V_s} = \frac{I_s}{I_p}$$

Transformers can come in many sizes and be used in many ways; they have provided a vital component for the electrical supply industry. According to Ohm's law, resistance decreases when voltage increases—and current decreases—therefore electrical substations use transformers to increase the voltage to allow less energy to be lost through resistance. Once the electrical current reaches a home, a step-down transformer outside the house decreases the voltage to the normal 120 volts used within homes.

SUMMARY

In 1831, Michael Faraday demonstrated electromagnetic induction by wrapping two coils of wire around the same metal ring. When the current in one coil was turned on and off, a current was induced in the second coil through the process of mutual inductance. This discovery came 10 years after Ørsted's finding of the magnetic field produced by a current-carrying wire, during which time Faraday reviewed the current research on electromagnetism and conducted many experiments. Continuing experimentation showed that any changing magnetic field could cause current to flow, and Faraday used his research to build the dynamo—the first generator that converted mechanical energy into electrical energy.

EMF is another term to describe the potential difference given to charges to allow them to flow similar to potential difference and voltage, but it is often used to specifically refer to the potential difference that a changing magnetic field produces. The term can be misleading as EMF is not a force, but the term was coined before electricity was fully understood. The amount of EMF produced is directly proportional to the strength of the magnetic field, the length of the wire, and the relative velocity between the wire and the magnets.

This induced EMF can be used for many different applications, such as flashlights that are shaken to charge a capacitor, allowing them to run without batteries for a time. Microphones also use this property when sound waves cause a diaphragm with a metal coil to vibrate within a magnetic field, inducing current to flow. To convert mechanical energy into electrical energy, generators have a drive shaft that turns an armature within a magnetic field, thus causing current to flow through the wires. The armature in generators produces alternating current as a result of the reversal of the coil's position within the magnetic fields every half rotation.

Lenz's law states that current induced through electromagnetic induction is always oriented to oppose the change or motion that created it. For example, in a generator, the armature moves within a magnetic field, producing current within the armature. The current through the armature then produces a second magnetic field that opposes the change caused in the first. This second magnetic field produces a force resistive to the armature's motion, which causes some of the inputted mechanical energy to be wasted in overcoming the force and not converted into electrical energy. The law also works when current produces a magnetic field, such as in motors. In a motor, the magnetic field produced by the current-carrying wire induces an opposing current through the wire, thus causing the net current to be less.

Two solenoids sharing a core can produce mutual inductance, whereby the changing current in the primary coil creates a changing magnetic field that induces a current in the secondary coil. Transformers use this to change the voltage of the electrical charge through adjusting the number of turns in each coil. Step-up transformers increase the voltage and decrease the current by having a greater number of turns in the secondary coil. A step-down transformer does the opposite; it decreases voltage and increases current by having a smaller secondary coil. Power companies use step-up transformers before electricity enters power lines to increase the voltage in order to decrease the resistance and use step-down transformers before electricity enters home to lower the voltage to a safe value.

Electromagnetism was born through Ørsted's demonstration that electrical current produces magnetism, Faraday's proof that changing magnetic fields induce electrical current, and Maxwell's four equations unifying it all mathematically. As one of the four fundamental forces, electromagnetism greatly impacts the world in large ways, such as cars, and in small ways, such as attraction and repulsion between the charged particles in an atom.

8

Conclusion

Electricity and magnetism, together often called *electromagnetism*, are responsible for the interactions of objects from the microscopic interactions of protons and electrons in atoms to the macroscopic interactions of books resting on a shelf. To understand how they react and respond to each other, electricity and magnetism must first be understood separately. Once the basic nature of these two components of the world are better appreciated, their unification can be explained.

The two types of electricity—static and current—both involve charged particles, most typically electrons because they are easily removed from an atom, but sometimes they involve the ions of molecules that have lost or gained electrons through chemical reactions, leaving them with a positive or negative charge. Static electricity involves the buildup of charged particles in a specific location. This buildup causes an imbalance of charge within an object. The imbalance is often caused when one material transfers electrons to another as a result of that material having a stronger attraction to electrons than the other. Materials that are conductors rarely sustain static electricity as they allow electrons to freely flow, thus preventing any accumulation from occurring. Insulators are materials that do not allow electrons to flow and are typically responsible for static electricity.

Static electricity can be generated in one of three ways: (1) charging by friction, (2) charging by conduction, or (3) charging by induction. When charged by friction, two objects of different materials are rubbed together—like socks rubbing against carpet—which causes electrons to transfer from one object to the other. This transfer of electrons causes one object to be negatively charged while the other is positively charged. Charging by conduction is when one charged object is brought into contact with a neutral object, allowing the buildup of charges to flow into the new object as they spread out as much as possible. This process leaves the previously neutral object with the same charge as the originally charged object. An object is charged by induction when a charged object is brought in close proximity to it, repelling the similar charges within the object and attracting the opposite charges. This charge can be maintained after the original object is removed by grounding the newly charged object and thus allowing the repelled charges to disperse into the Earth. Based on the fact that like charges repel, only so much static electricity can be produced before discharge occurs when some charges jump from one location to another.

The easiest way to detect whether an object has become charged is by bringing it near an object with a known charge. If the first object remains motionless, it has no charge; however, attraction or repulsion to the second object indicates a charge and can indicate whether the charge is negative or positive. Coulomb's law shows the relationship between the magnitude of the charge on two objects, the distance between them, and the resulting attractive or repulsive force. Using this law allows for the calculation of any of these measurements as long as the others are known. Knowing this information can be important because static electricity is used in many applications, such as printers and fly traps.

Both static and current electricity share some properties because both involve charged particles—whether they are moving or not. Electric fields are the areas around any charged particle in which the attractive and repulsive forces exerted on other charged particles can be felt. Electric field lines can be drawn to show where the field is strongest—typically between two opposite charges—or weakest—such as between two like charges. Scientists have used electric fields in many different experiments, but most notably Robert Millikan used them in his oil drop experiment to determine the exact charge of a single electron. Charged particles within an electric field, whether they are gathered in one location or are flowing through a wire, all have electric potential energy. This energy is the ability of the force exerted by the electric field to do work on the particles by moving them. Because this energy is also dependent on the magnitude of the charge within the field, discussing the electric potential difference, a measurement of the change in the potential energy per unit charge within an electric field, to describe an electric field is typically more practical. This electric potential difference is also called *voltage* or *electromotive force* when it is created by a magnetic field.

When a conductor gains excess charges, the charges spread out to produce the least amount of repulsion possible and quickly reach electrostatic equilibrium in which there is no potential difference between the charges. Conductors in this state have an electric field perpendicular to the charged surface, which is strongest in areas in which the surfaces are the most curved. In addition, because there is no electric field beneath the surface of the conductor, a closed conductor can act as a protective cage, thus keeping electric fields and forces out. Capacitors are used to store electrical energy in such a way that it can be released slowly over time or released in one or two large bursts. Capacitors are made by placing an insulator between two metal plates. The insulating material determines how much charge the capacitor is able to store.

Current electricity occurs when electrons flow through a closed path that results from a potential difference between the start and finish of this path. However, electrical energy must be used to keep this potential difference in place because the electrons flow in an effort to negate it. There are several different methods used to add this electrical energy. Electrochemical cells—more typically called *batteries*—convert chemical energy stored within the bonds between atoms into electrical energy, allowing current to flow. These cells can be either dry or wet, depending on whether the electrolyte used within the cell is a paste or a liquid. Photovoltaic cells convert light into electrical energy through the use of photosensitive materials that give off electrons when struck by light. Mechanical energy can be converted into electrical energy through piezoelectric crystals, which produce a potential difference when these crystals are hit or squeezed. A final way to produce electrical energy is through generators that use electromagnetic induction.

There are many ways other than voltage to measure the electricity flowing through an electrical path. For example, current indicates how fast the electrons are moving. Ohm's law also introduces resistance, which measures a material's natural resistance to the flow of electrons. The law relates voltage, current, and resistance and shows that voltage and current are directly proportional, whereas an increase in resistance causes a decrease in current. The electrical power used can also be measured to show the rate at which electrical work is done. Power can be calculated by using either the classical mechanics equation of work over time or by multiplying current and voltage. As electrons flow through any material, some resistance encountered allows electrical energy to be converted to heat. This conversion in some devices, such as heaters and stoves, is purposeful because the production of heat is the goal of the device.

The electrical path through which current electricity flows is called a *circuit*. A circuit can contain components in series or in parallel with each other, or it can contain a combination of the two. Components in series with each other share the same path so that if one device breaks, none of the devices work. When objects are placed in a circuit in parallel to each other, they are in separate paths so that electrons can flow to each device separately. The current that flows through a circuit can be either alternating current (AC), which flows back and forth between directions, or direct current (DC), which flows in one direction only.

There are many different possible components within a circuit, each of which has its own unique symbol for circuit diagrams. Circuit diagrams are drawn a specific way so that any person can look at the diagram and determine what components are used and how they are installed within the circuit. All circuits must contain a conductive path—wires—and a voltage source, such as a battery or generator. Beyond these two components, a circuit can contain any number of devices, depending on what the circuit is designed to accomplish. Many circuits need to produce light through the use of either light bulbs or the brighter and more efficient light-emitting diodes. Some circuits use transistors to increase the current flowing through them. Resistors can be used to decrease the current to protect devices that may be easily harmed by high currents. Color codes on the body of resistors help to identify their resistance. Grounds are used in circuits to provide a path for the harmless dissipation of excess electrons. Different meters can be included in a circuit to measure its current and resistance; however, they must be installed correctly, depending on what they are measuring—that is, in parallel to measure voltage and in series to measure current.

There are several devices used in circuits to prevent damage and to protect devices from too much voltage or current. One cause of too much current is a short circuit in which a circuit becomes shortened as a result of a connection where there should not be one—such as when insulation becomes worn or eaten away—and the resistance is too low, allowing the flow of high current that could cause overheating and a possible fire. Fuses can be used to prevent this condition because they contain a thin piece of metal that melts when current becomes too high, thus opening the circuit before more damage occurs. The problem with fuses is that they must be replaced every time they overheat; therefore, circuit breakers are used in homes and businesses instead. In a circuit breaker, the increased current causes a switch to open and thus stops the flow of electrons. Instead of replacing the switch, it can just be closed once the problem has been located. Ground fault interrupters are also important safety devices that protect against shocks. When a ground fault interrupter detects a change in the returning current, most likely caused by an extra path (e.g., water), the circuit is opened, making these devices important to have in places where water is likely to accumulate, such as kitchens and bathrooms.

Kirchhoff's circuit laws describe the relationships between current and voltage and explain how devices are connected within a circuit. The first law says that the total current flowing into a junction is the same as the total current flowing out of it, whereas the second law states that the voltage supplied by the source is equal to the sum of the voltages used by the devices within one loop of the circuit. These two laws help determine why series circuits have the same current, but different voltages, at every location. However, the sum of the voltages used by each component within the series adds up to the voltage delivered by the battery, or other source. The equivalent resistance—total resistance of the circuit—is equal to the sum of the resistances of each component. In a parallel circuit, the voltage is the same at each component, whereas the current differs, with the total current being used as equal to the total current for the circuit. In a parallel circuit, the reciprocal of the equivalent resistance is equal to the sum of the reciprocals of each component's resistance.

Series circuits are more practical for small circuits within electronic devices because of the limitation that any malfunctioning part causes the entire circuit to stop working. These circuits typically cost less to produce because they use less wiring and have the advantage of supplying a uniform current. Parallel circuits deliver maximum voltage to each component and continue to work even if one part malfunctions. However, most large-scale circuits are complex because they contain some components in series and others in parallel. This complexity is particularly true with safety features, such as fuses and circuit breakers, because they must be in series with the entire circuit that they are trying to protect.

Magnets are relatively simple in comparison, although some of their properties are similar to those of electricity. A magnet contains many domains in which the unpaired electrons within the atoms are all spinning the same way, creating tiny magnetic fields that reinforce each other to create one detectable magnetic field. Some materials, such as metal, are magnetized more easily by either being in contact with another magnet or by being rubbed with one. A magnet has two poles—the north pole and the south pole—in which the magnetic field is the strongest. Like poles will repel each other, whereas opposite poles will attract each other; however, the two poles can never be separated—cutting a magnet in half only results in two smaller magnets. The magnetic field is the area around the magnet in which these attractive and repulsive forces can be felt.

Despite their apparent differences, there were scientists who believed that electricity and magnetism originated from the same source. One of these scientists, Hans Christian Ørsted, discovered the first link between these two forces when he showed that a current-carrying wire produces a circular magnetic field around the wire. Coiling a wire also was shown to make this magnetic field strong enough to produce an electromagnet—a magnet produced by electricity. In addition, when a current-carrying wire or even just a single charged particle is placed in a magnetic field, the magnetic field that they produce reacts with the original field to either attract or repel the wire or particle.

Right-hand rules were developed for electromagnetism to help determine the direction of a force or a current. The first right-hand rule shows the direction of the magnetic field around a current-carrying wire through imagining that the wire is held in the right hand with the thumb pointing in the direction of conventional current. The magnetic field produced curls around the wire in the same direction as the fingers. The second right-hand rule is used to determine the location of the poles of an electromagnet through picturing the electromagnet held in the right hand with the fingers wrapping around it in the direction of conventional current. The thumb then points to the north pole of the electromagnet. The third and final right-hand rule can illustrate the direction of the force exerted on a wire or positive particle within a magnetic field. One can do this by visualizing the right hand held flat with the fingers pointing along the magnetic field and the thumb pointing in the direction of conventional current through the wire or the velocity of the particle so that the palm of the hand shows the direction of the force.

Scientists quickly saw the value of electromagnetism and began developing it for use in new devices, such as the galvanometer. A galvanometer uses the force between an electromagnet and a permanent magnet to deflect a needle along a scale to measure current. Speakers contain cones with wires wrapped around their base to create an electromagnet when current passes through them. The base of this cone is surrounded by a permanent magnet, and the attraction and repulsion that is felt as the current changes magnitude and direction pushes and pulls the speaker cone to create sound waves in the air. An electric motor uses electrical energy to produce mechanical energy by creating an electromagnet and by using the attractive and repulsive forces between it and a nearby permanent magnet to cause the electromagnet—often called an *armature* in a motor—to spin.

It was another 10 years after the discovery of electromagnetism that the next link between electricity and magnetism was revealed in the form of electromagnetic induction—the production of electrical current in a wire caused by a changing magnetic field. This magnetic field could be changing in strength—perhaps caused by a varying current that is producing this field—or the electrical wire and magnet could be moving relative to each other. The voltage produced in a wire caused by electromagnetic induction is often called *electromotive force*. Its magnitude is dependent on the strength of the magnetic field, the length of the wire, and the velocity at which the wire is moving.

This induced voltage is used in many different applications, including flashlights that use the motion of a coil of wire in and out of a magnetic field, instead of a battery, to produce electrical energy. Microphones use the motion of a coil attached to a thin diaphragm when sound waves strike it to convert sound into electricity. Generators are devices that convert mechanical energy into electrical energy. As an armature is turned within a magnetic field, electrical current is created in a manner that is almost exactly the opposite of how motors function. The current produced by a generator fluctuates between the maximum possible—when the electromagnet and the magnetic field are perpendicular to each other—to no current at all—when the electromagnet is parallel to the magnetic field. Lenz's law can be used to determine the direction of the current produced through electromotive induction. It states that the current produced is always in a direction necessary to oppose the change in the magnetic field that created it—through the magnetic field that the new current produces.

Transformers are used to change the voltage of an electrical current through mutual inductance in which one coil of wire produces a changing magnetic field that induces a current to flow in a second coil of wire. The ratio of primary to secondary coils determines whether the secondary voltage is higher or lower. A step-up transformer goes from less primary coils to more secondary coils with an increase in voltage and a decrease in resistance. A step-down transformer has more primary coils than it does secondary coils with a lower secondary voltage and a higher secondary resistance. These devices are invaluable to the electrical supply industry because they allow electrical current to be altered to provide the least resistance while traveling long distances through power lines.

This unification of electricity and magnetism was a first step to a possible theory of everything to show that all forces come from the same place and follow the same rules. Maxwell's equations further developed this unification mathematically, even adding in optics as light was found to be a form of electromagnetic radiation. Next, Albert Einstein unified parts of classical mechanics and electromagnetism with special and general relativity. He spent the rest of his life attempting to unify all areas of physics with no success. Since then, many physicists have continued his search, and many ideas—such as string theory—are being considered, but none has yet been mathematically or theoretically proven.

SI Units and Conversions

UNIT	QUANTITY	SYMBOL	CONVERSION
Base Units			
meter	length	m	1 m = 3.2808 feet
kilogram	mass	kg	1 kg = 2.205 pounds
second	time	s	
ampere	electric current	A	
kelvin	thermodynamic temperature	K	1 K = 1°C = 1.8°F
candela	luminous intensity		
mole	amount of substance	d mol	
Supplementary Units			
radian	plane angle	rad	π / 2 rad = 90°
steradian	solid angle	sr	
Derived Units			
coulomb	quantity of electricity	C	
cubic meter	volume	m^3	1 m^3 = 1.308 yards^3
farad	capacitance	F	
henry	inductance	H	
hertz	frequency	Hz	
joule	energy	J	1 J = 0.2389 calories
kilogram per cubic meter	density	kg m^{-3}	1 kg m^{-3} = 0.0624 lb. ft^{-3}
lumen	luminous flux	lm	
lux	illuminance	lx	
meter per second	speed	m s^{-1}	1 m s^{-1} = 3.281 ft s^{-1}

UNIT	QUANTITY	SYMBOL	CONVERSION
meter per second squared	acceleration	$m\ s^{-2}$	
mole per cubic meter	concentration	$mol\ m^{-3}$	
newton	force	N	1 N = 7.218 lb. force
ohm	electric resistance	Ω	
pascal	pressure	Pa	$1\ Pa = \dfrac{0.145\ lb}{in^{-2}}$
radian per second	angular velocity	$rad\ s^{-1}$	
radian per second squared	angular acceleration	$rad\ s^{-2}$	
square meter	area	m^2	$1\ m^2 = 1.196\ yards^2$
tesla	magnetic flux density	T	
volt	electromotive force	V	
watt	power	W	$1W = 3.412\ Btu\ h^{-1}$
weber	magnetic flux	Wb	

PREFIXES USED WITH SI UNITS		
PREFIX	SYMBOL	VALUE
atto	a	$\times 10^{-18}$
femto	f	$\times 10^{-15}$
pico	p	$\times 10^{-12}$
nano	n	$\times 10^{-9}$
micro	μ	$\times 10^{-6}$
milli	m	$\times 10^{-3}$
centi	c	$\times 10^{-2}$
deci	d	$\times 10^{-1}$
deca	da	$\times 10$
hecto	h	$\times 10^{2}$
kilo	k	$\times 10^{3}$
mega	M	$\times 10^{6}$
giga	G	$\times 10^{9}$
tera	T	$\times 10^{12}$

PHYSICS PRINCIPLES

The following information serves as a reference to provide additional information on important topics and further understanding of the material covered in this book. It includes brief explanations of the laws, theories, and major concepts covered in this book. It lists the chapter in which the topic is first introduced, although later chapters may also reference it. Every chapter may not be referenced because not all chapters introduce a major theory or concept.

KIRCHHOFF'S CIRCUIT LAWS (CHAPTER 5)

Gustav Kirchhoff used two circuit laws to summarize how current and voltage are affected by the construction of the electrical circuit. Kirchhoff's first law—sometimes called Kirchhoff's current law or Kirchhoff's junction rule—states that the total current flowing away from a junction is equal to the total current flowing into it. This law may seem somewhat obvious in accordance with conservation laws because there cannot be less or more charges after a junction. This law helps explain that if an electrical path splits into several paths, the current in each path is less, whereas if several paths combine into one, the final current is the sum of the currents from the original paths. This law provides the foundation of most types of circuit simulation software, which are designed to find faults with circuits before they are constructed.

Kirchhoff's second law—also called *Kirchhoff's voltage law* or *Kirchhoff's loop rule*—states that the sum of the voltage provided in any closed loop is equal to the sum of the voltage drops within the same loop. Kirchhoff's second law is an application of the law of conservation of energy to electrical circuits—electrical devices cannot use energy that is not available. It explains that paths within a circuit will all have the same voltage within their paths, regardless of the number of paths. One limitation of this law is when the circuit is in the presence of a fluctuating magnetic field, which would induce additional voltage within the circuit. Electrical engineering widely uses these two laws because precise values of current and voltage are needed at specific locations within a circuit.

FOUR FUNDAMENTAL FORCES (CHAPTER 6)

Our world is ruled by all kinds of interactions between different types of matter. These interactions are caused by one of the four fundamental forces—gravity, electromagnetism, weak nuclear force, and strong nuclear force. Gravity is the attraction that any object has on another object. The strength of the force depends on the distance between the two objects and the masses of the objects. This force causes things to fall toward the ground, planets to orbit the sun, and the tides on our beaches. Electromagnetism is seen in the forces between charged particles and the forces exerted by magnets. Both gravity and electromagnetism can be felt at an infinite distance, although the forces do get weaker with added distance. Weak nuclear force and strong nuclear force are both very short-ranged forces and are felt within the atom. Weak nuclear force is responsible for radioactive decay, which is the stabilization of nuclei by the emission of particles and energy. The strong nuclear force is the force that holds protons and neutrons together in the nucleus of an atom. This force overcomes the electromagnetic repulsion that exists between particles of like charges.

FARADAY'S LAW OF INDUCTION (CHAPTER 7)

Faraday's law of induction explains that a changing magnetic field induces an electrical current to flow through a wire within that field. Specifically, it states that the induced electromotive force (EMF) is proportional to the rate of change of the magnetic flux. Magnetic flux is a measurement that describes the amount of magnetic field passing through a given surface and is proportional to the number of magnetic field lines passing through the surface. Magnetic flux is proportional to the strength of the magnetic field and the area of the surface, and is also affected by the angle between the surface and the direction of the magnetic field, where magnetic fields traveling parallel to the surface have no flux. The symbol used to represent magnetic flux is phi, Φ. Faraday's law of induction is unique in that it describes two different phenomena, with EMF being induced due either to motion of the wire or to the magnetic field changing. Though the law covers both of these situations, different equations are used in either situation to determine the magnitude of the EMF produced. This double nature eventually helped lead the famous German physicist Albert Einstein (1879-1955) to his theory of special relativity.

WORK-ENERGY THEOREM (CHAPTER 7)

The work-energy theorem states that the work done on an object is equal to its change in kinetic energy. For example, when a father pushes his child on the swings, the work he does in pushing the child is equal to their change in kinetic energy. The more force and work he puts in, the more the child's speed increases. Work can also be done to decrease kinetic energy. When an ice skater coasts to a stop, the work done on the skater by the frictional force of the ice is equal to the skater's change in kinetic energy. When work is done in the opposite direction of a starting velocity, the kinetic energy decreases as the speed decreases. Work can have an affect on potential energy as well when the work is due to the force of gravity or the work moves a charged particle. Imagine a wire being moved through a magnetic field. The work being done to move the charges within the wire increases their electric potential energy.

MAXWELL'S EQUATIONS (CHAPTER 7)

James Clerk Maxwell (1831–79) was the Scottish physicist who unified electricity, magnetism, and optics through his development of electromagnetism. Maxwell's four differential equations describe electric and magnetic fields, their creation, and their interactions. Through his equations, Maxwell summarized years of research by scientists regarding electricity and magnetism, although his own addition added the key that unified it all. The first of Maxwell's equations, called Gauss's law, states that the electric field generated is influenced by the number of charges within the object. It also shows the direction that electric field lines travel from positive to negative charges. Applying this law to electric point charges allows for the derivation of Coulomb's law, which had already been published previously. Gauss's law for magnetism, Maxwell's second equation, mathematically shows that there is no magnetic charge and that it is not possible to isolate a single magnetic pole. This law also states that magnetic field lines have no beginning or end; they travel in loops or travel indefinitely.

Maxwell's third equation is based on Faraday's law of induction, which expresses that a changing magnetic field induces an electric field, thus causing current to flow. Maxwell's fourth and final equation is Ampère's law with one important correction from Maxwell. Ampère's original law stated that magnetic fields could be produced by electrical currents; Maxwell's correction added that they could also be produced by electric fields. This addition is so important because it allows for the existence of electromagnetic radiation—self-sustaining electric and magnetic fields. This equation also allows for the calculation of this electromagnetic radiation, which proved to be the same as the previously calculated speed of light. Maxwell's equations impacted physics dramatically, helping to lead to the theories of general and special relativity and providing a foundation for the fields of electrodynamics and quantum mechanics.

LENZ'S LAW (CHAPTER 7)

Lenz's law asserts that the electromotive force (EMF) generated by a change in magnetic flux is always oriented in a way to produce a new magnetic field that opposes this change. For example, if the decrease in a magnetic field induces current, the direction of the current will be such that the magnetic field produced by the current will be in the same direction as the original magnetic field to oppose the field's decrease in strength. If the current is caused by an increase in the magnetic field, the direction of the current will produce a new magnetic field in the opposite direction of the original to oppose this increase. The equations derived from Faraday's law of induction calculate the magnitude of the EMF generated, whereas Lenz's law finds the direction of the EMF and the resulting current.

GLOSSARY

ALTERNATING CURRENT (AC)   An electric current that regularly changes direction with a magnitude that varies similar to a sine wave.

CAPACITANCE   A measurement that is the ratio of the charge on one of the conductive plates of a capacitor to the potential difference between the two plates. Capacitance is measured in farads (F).

CAPACITOR   An electrical device used to store electrical charge to be released later over time or in large bursts.

CHARGING BY CONDUCTION   A way to produce static electricity in an object through contact with another charged object. The charged particles spread into the new object, giving it the same, but weaker, charge as the originally charged object.

CHARGING BY FRICTION   A way to produce static electricity in an object by rubbing it with an object made of different material. The material with a higher attraction for electrons will strip them from the other material, creating one positively charged object and one negatively charged object.

CHARGING BY INDUCTION   A way to produce static electricity in an object by bringing a charged item close to the object. The charged item repels like charges and attracts opposite charges within the object.

CIRCUIT BREAKER   A safety device used in circuits that opens the circuit whenever the current becomes too high as a way to prevent overheating and electrical fires.

CONDUCTOR   An object that allows electrons to flow through it, spreading them evenly along its surface.

CURRENT ELECTRICITY   The type of electricity in which charge flows through a path.

DIRECT CURRENT (DC)   An electrical current that flows in the same direction with little or no variation in magnitude.

DOMAIN   A region within a ferromagnetic material with a singular polarity caused by the unpaired electrons in the atoms all spinning the same direction and creating one magnetic field. The orientation of the domains within a material determines its magnetic properties.

ELECTRIC CURRENT The rate at which electrons flow through an electrical path. Electric current is measured in amperes (A).

ELECTRIC FIELD A field that surrounds charged objects, exerting attractive and repulsive forces on other charged objects within it. The strength of an electric field is measured by the force exerted per unit of charge in newtons per coulomb (N/C).

ELECTRIC POTENTIAL DIFFERENCE A measurement of the change in potential energy per unit charge within an electric field. Electric potential difference is also called *voltage* and *electromotive force* and is measured in volts (V).

ELECTRIC POTENTIAL ENERGY The potential energy of a charged object as a result of its location within an electric field. Electric potential energy is measured in joules (J).

ELECTRIC POWER The rate at which electrical energy is transferred. Electric power is measured in watts (W).

ELECTROCHEMICAL CELL A device that converts the chemical energy stored within bonds into electrical energy. Many electrochemical cells together are called a battery.

ELECTROMAGNET A coil of wire that becomes a magnet when electrical current passes through it. An electromagnet is also called a *solenoid* or an *armature.*

ELECTROMAGNETIC INDUCTION The process of generating an electrical current in a conductive path resulting from the changing magnetic field around it.

ELECTROMOTIVE FORCE (EMF) A measurement of the change in potential energy per unit charge within an electric field, frequently used when the change is produced through electromagnetic induction. Electromotive force is also called *voltage* and *electric potential difference* and is measured in volts (V).

ELECTRONS The negatively charged elementary particle found outside of the nucleus of an atom.

EQUIVALENT RESISTANCE The total resistance of an entire circuit. In a series circuit, equivalent resistance is the sum of the individual resistances, and in a parallel circuit, the reciprocal of this is the sum of the reciprocals of the individual resistances. Equivalent resistance is measured in ohms (Ω).

FIRST RIGHT-HAND RULE   This rule is used to determine the direction of a magnetic field around a straight, current-carrying wire. Holding the wire in the right hand with the thumb pointing in the direction of conventional current and the fingers wrapped around the wire shows the direction of the magnetic field.

FUSE   A safety device that consists of a thin piece of metal designed to melt when the current becomes too high, protecting the circuit from overheating.

GROUND   An electrical path between a circuit and the Earth or a large conducting body. A ground is used to prevent the buildup of excess charge.

GROUND FAULT INTERRUPTER   A safety device that detects small changes in returning current that may be caused by additional conductive paths, such as water, and quickly opens the circuit.

INSULATOR   A material that does not allow electrons to flow easily through it.

KILOWATT-HOUR (kWh)   A measurement of electrical energy delivered that is equal to 1,000 watts delivered for 1 hour.

LIGHT-EMITTING DIODES   A diode that emits light when electrical current passes through it. Light-emitting diodes are brighter and more energy efficient than incandescent lights.

MAGNETIC FIELD   The area surrounding a magnet in which attractive and repulsive forces are exerted on other magnets.

MUTUAL INDUCTANCE   The process by which two electrical coils share a core and the changing current of the first coil creates a changing magnetic field that induces a current in the second coil. This process is used by transformers to change the voltage of electrical current.

NEUTRONS The neutral elementary particle found within the nucleus of an atom.

PARALLEL CIRCUIT An electrical circuit with two or more paths through which charges can flow.

PHOTOVOLTAIC CELL A device that converts electromagnetic radiation into electrical energy.

PIEZOELECTRIC EFFECT A property of some materials through which they produce an electrical current when they experience mechanical stress and mechanically stress when an electrical current is applied.

PROTONS The positively charged elementary particle found within the nucleus of an atom.

RESISTANCE The property of conductive materials that slows the flow of electrons, converting electrical energy into heat. Resistance is measured in ohms (Ω).

RESISTOR A device used in an electrical circuit to increase the resistance of that electrical path.

SECOND RIGHT-HAND RULE This rule is used to show the direction of the magnetic field produced by an electromagnet. With the electromagnet held in the right hand with the fingers wrapped around the coils in the same direction as conventional current, the thumb points to the north pole of the magnet.

SERIES CIRCUIT An electrical circuit with one path through which charges can flow.

SHORT CIRCUIT A usually accidental path of low resistance within a circuit that creates a high current.

STATIC ELECTRICITY The type of electricity in which charge accumulates in one location.

THIRD RIGHT-HAND RULE This rule is used to determine the direction of a force on a current-carrying wire or a positively charged particle within a magnetic field. With the right hand open, the fingers pointing in the direction of the magnetic field, and the thumb in the direction of conventional current or velocity of the particle, the palm of the hand shows the direction of the force.

TRANSISTOR A semiconductor device that increases or decreases current without much energy loss.

VOLTAGE A measurement of the change in potential energy per unit charge within an electric field. Voltage is also called *electric potential difference* and *electromotive force* and is measured in volts (V).

FURTHER RESOURCES

Print and Internet

American Physical Society. "Renewable Energy and the Electricity Grid." *ScienceDaily*, November 16, 2010. Available online. URL: www.sciencedaily.com/releases/2010/11/101116093530.htm. Accessed January 18, 2011. This article describes the American Physical Society's report on how to integrate renewable energy into the U.S. grid system for distributing electricity.

Balaram, P. "The Trouble with Science." *Current Science* 99.5: 553–554, September 2010. Available online. URL: www.ias.ac.in/currsci/10 sep2010/553.pdf. Accessed February 22, 2011. The author explains how Maxwell's equations have led to a drive for the unification of all of physics.

Caputi, Angel. "How Do Electric Eels Generate a Voltage and Why Do They Not Get Shocked in the Process?" *Scientific American*, December 5, 2005. Available online. URL: www.scientificamerican.com/article.cfm?id=how-do-electric-eels-gene. Accessed January 6, 2011. This article explains how an electric eel produces an electric shock and why the water around it does not transmit the shock back to the eel.

Chartterjee, Sabyasachi. "Michael Faraday: Discovery of Electromagnetic Induction." *Resonance* 7.3:35–45, March 2002. Available online. URL: www.ias.ac.in/resonance/Mar2002/pdf/Mar2002p35-45.pdf. Accessed February 21, 2011. This article describes Michael Faraday's discovery of electromagnetic induction, including the research done by other scientists that led to his findings and the impact that it had.

De Pree, Christopher Gordon. *Physics Made Simple*. New York: Broadway Books, 2004. This book gives a basic introduction to most physics topics, including electricity and magnetism.

Dreier, David. *Electrical Circuits: Harnessing Electricity*. Minneapolis: Compass Point Books, 2008. This short book describes the different types of electrical circuits and explains how they are used in citywide electrical grids and in homes.

Ferris, Julie. *Ideas That Change the World*. New York: DK Publishing, 2010. This book discusses some of the big ideas that led to the invention of items that have changed the world, including the ball point pen and the battery.

Flowers, Charles. *Instability Rules: The Ten Most Amazing Ideas of Modern Science*. New York: John Wiley & Sons, Inc., 2002. This book provides an interesting and easily understood description of ten important principles of modern science and their impact.

Fraunhofer-Gesellschaft. "Conductor Paths for Marvelous Light." *ScienceDaily*, November 21, 2010. Available online. URL: www.science daily.com/releases/2010/11/101118084431.htm. Accessed January 31, 2011. This article discusses the new field of organic light-emitting diodes, explains how they could be used to improve lighting options, and describes the current problems that they present.

Glatzmaier, Gary A. "What Causes the Periodic Reversals of the Earth's Magnetic Field? Have There Been Any Successful Attempts to Model the Phenomenon?" *Scientific American*, October 21, 1999. Available online. URL: www.scientificamerican.com/article.cfm ?id=what-causes-the-periodic. Accessed February 15, 2011. The author explains one theory on why the Earth's magnetic field periodically changes and describes the results of a recent computer model that indicates what might happen when it occurs again.

Johnson, George. *The Ten Most Beautiful Experiments*. New York: Alferd A. Knopf, 2008. The author describes and explains ten of the most important and fascinating experiments ever conducted.

Knier, Gil. "How Do Photovoltaics Work?" April 5, 2010. Available online. URL: science.nasa.gov/science-news/science-at-nasa/2002/ solarcells/. Accessed January 13, 2011. This online article explains how solar cells convert energy from the Sun into electrical energy.

Mardiguian, Michel. *Electrostatic Discharge: Understand, Simulate and Fix ESD Problems*. Hoboken: John Wiley & Sons, Inc., 2009. The author discusses the causes of electrostatic discharge and its effect on electronics and explains how to prevent it from occurring.

Ohm, Georg, and Thomas Dixon Lockwood. *The Galvanic Circuit Investigated Mathematically (1891)*. Whitefish: Kessinger Publishing, LLC, 2009. This book is a reprint of Georg Ohm's book with contributions from Thomas Lockwood on Ohm's research into the relationship between current, voltage, and resistance in electric circuits, which led to the development of Ohm's law.

Pickrell, John. "A new way to stick it to flies." *Science News* 161.8:126, February 23, 2002. This article describes research into using static charge to create traps for flies.

Reid, T. R. *The Chip: How Two Americans Invented the Microchip and Launched a Revolution*. New York: Random House, 2001. The author describes the research done by Jack Kilby and Robert Noyce to develop the silicon microchip and to make computers smaller and more affordable for the average person.

Rupke, Edward J. "What Happens When Lightning Strikes an Airplane?" *Scientific American*, August 14, 2006. Available online. URL: www.scientificamerican.com/article.cfm?id=what-happens-when-lightni. Accessed January 7, 2011. The author explains what happens to an airplane when it is struck by lightning.

Technische Universitaet Muenchen. "Electric Current Moves Magnetic Vortices: With the Help of Neutrons, Physicists Discover New Ways to Save Data." *ScienceDaily*, December, 21 2010. Available online. URL: www.sciencedaily.com/releases/2010/12/101217145653.htm. Accessed February 15, 2011. This article summarizes research on using the spin and magnetic moment of electrons to store data in a fast and efficient manner.

Tsuda, Takao. *Electric Field Applications in Chromatography, Industrial and Chemical Processes*. New York: John Wiley & Sons, Inc., 2008. This book describes current uses for electrical fields in such applications as chromatography—the separation of different chemicals within a compound—and other chemical and industrial processes.

Web Sites

How Stuff Works. Available online. URL: www.howstuffworks.com/. Accessed December 1, 2010. This Web site simplifies and explains how a variety of items work from seeing-eye dog training to televisions.

HyperPhysics. Available online. URL: hyperphysics.phy-astr.gsu.edu/hbase/hph.html. Accessed December 6, 2010. This Web site is run by the Department of Physics and Astronomy at Georgia State University. It covers a multitude of physics topics in a straightforward and easily understood manner.

The Physics Classroom. Available online. URL: www.physicsclassroom.com/. Accessed January 6, 2011. This Web site is designed to aid high school physics students with their understanding of physics concepts through simple language and supporting graphics.

INDEX